Victorian Poetry in Context

Texts and Contexts

Series Editors: Gail Ashton and Fiona McCulloch

Texts and Contexts is a series of clear, concise and accessible introductions to key literary fields and concepts. The series provides the literary, critical, historical context for texts and authors in a specific literary area in a way that introduces a range of work in the field and enables further independent study and reading.

Other titles available in the series:

Medieval English Romance in Context, Gail Ashton
Postcolonial Literatures in Context, Julie Mullaney
The Contemporary American Novel in Context, Andrew Dix, Brian Jarvis and Paul Jenner
Children's Literature in Context, Fiona McCulloch
The Victorian Novel in Context, Grace Moore

Victorian Poetry in Context

Texts and Contexts

ROSIE MILES

B L O O M S B U R Y

LONDON · NEW DELHI · NEW YORK · SYDNEY

Bloomsbury Academic
An imprint of Bloomsbury Publishing Plc

50 Bedford Square   1385 Broadway
London   New York
WC1B 3DP   NY 10018
UK   USA

www.bloomsbury.com

First published 2013

British Library Cataloguing-in-Publication Data
A catalogue record for this book is available from the British Library.

ISBN: HB: 978-0-8264-3055-7
PB: 978-0-8264-3767-9
ePDF: 978-1-4411-8246-3
ePub: 978-1-4411-8851-9

Library of Congress Cataloging-in-Publication Data
Miles, Rosie, 1968-
Victorian poetry in context / Rosie Miles.
pages cm. – (Texts in Contexts)
ISBN 978-0-8264-3767-9 (pbk.) – ISBN 978-0-8264-3055-7 (hardcover) –
ISBN 978-1-4411-8246-3 (epdf) – ISBN 978-1-4411-8851-9 (epub)   1. English
poetry–19th century–History and criticism.   I. Title.
PR591.M55 2013
821'.809–dc23
2013000826

Typeset by Newgen Imaging Systems Pvt Ltd, Chennai, India
Printed and bound in Great Britain

*For my Victorian literature students, and all who work at
Gladstone's Library, Hawarden*

While critics don't need to be poets, and while poets don't have to be critics, each might well feel tempted by the beauties and powers of the other. All should mingle more.

MOLLY MCQUADE (2000)

Read for oneself, expose the mind bare to the poem, and transcribe in all its haste and imperfection whatever may be the result of the impact.

VIRGINIA WOOLF, on reading Christina Rossetti (1932)

'As to poetry, you know,' said Humpty Dumpty, stretching out one of his great hands, 'I can repeat poetry as well as other folk, if it comes to that –'
'Oh, it needn't come to that!' Alice hastily said, hoping to keep him from beginning.

Humpty Dumpty explaining 'Jabberwocky', in *Alice Through the Looking Glass* (1871)

Contents

CONTENTS

Series editors' preface

*T*exts and Contexts offers clear and accessible introductions to key literary fields. Each book in the series outlines major historical, social, cultural and literary contexts that impact upon its specified area. It engages contemporary responses to selected texts and authors through a variety of exemplary close readings, by exploring the ideas of seminal theorists and/or a range of critical approaches, as well as examining adaptations and afterlives. Readers are encouraged to make connections and ground further independent study through 'Review', 'Reading' and 'Research' sections at the end of most chapters, which offer selected bibliographies, web resources, open and closed questions, discussion topics and pointers for extended research.

Preface

When I was an undergraduate I was asked to read a poem by William Morris entitled 'The Haystack in the Floods' (1858). It begins with two rhetorical questions:

> Had she come all the way for this,
> To part at last without a kiss?
> Yea, had she borne the dirt and rain
> That her own eyes might see him slain
> Beside the haystack in the floods? (1–5)

The poem tells of a character called Jehane who is placed in a disturbingly entrapped position whereby she must 'yield as [the] paramour' (71) to one Godmar or her lover Robert 'will not see the rain leave off' (72). Jehane faces an impossible dilemma: she 'cannot choose but sin and sin' (95). Although there is narrative tension the poem repeatedly suggests that this tale is not going to end well, and the opening lines above are refracted into an erratic, intermittent refrain, which erupts into the poem's tetrameter (four beat) couplets like some numb return of the repressed. The psychological intensity of the situation writes itself through Jehane's body and her refusal to yield bespeaks an integrity and purity. It also unleashes an episode of violence that wouldn't be out of place in a film like *Reservoir Dogs* (1992).

I discovered that the poem was in dialogue with medieval sources, and read more about William Morris. I found a man of multiple talents, whose organic wallpaper and textile designs now adorn a hundred and one surfaces, and who was instrumental in establishing the Socialist movement in the 1880s. Throughout his varied career and commitments, poetry remained. I also discovered Pre-Raphaelite art, and during an exhibition of Pre-Raphaelite drawings heard a series of lectures on 'The Brotherhood'. Morris's opening inscription in his first volume – 'To my friend Dante Gabriel Rossetti – painter –

I dedicate these poems' – started to make sense. Poetry and painting frequently spoke to each other in the Victorian era.

My reason for starting here is that this Victorian poem had a profound influence on my life. At some level it helped shape subsequent decisions I made about what I was going to do with myself. This may be the kind of assertion of which some Victorian commentators on poetry would have heartily approved, as they strove to make sense of what poetry and the poet could mean in an era of increasingly utilitarian values. What place should poetry have in our national life? How can poetry speak to massive social change? Is there a 'proper' subject for poetry? If it speaks of the past, what is its relation to the present? What is the 'right' relationship between art and life?

This book considers the range and breadth of poetry written between 1830 and 1900. In-depth readings of specific poems feature in Part Two. The outer chapters contextualize Victorian poetry in wider social, cultural, intellectual and literary frameworks, as well as commenting on its critical fortunes and how Victorian poetry has lived on into the twentieth and twenty-first centuries. Ultimately it is poetry that gives life to everything written here and I hope this book will return the reader to the original poems, again and again.

I have assumed that readers could be accessing the Victorian poems discussed here in any number of different editions. The majority are available in the anthologies cited in the Bibliography. Line numbers from the poems are given after quotations throughout. Quotations followed by p. or pp. are taken from critical commentary.

Acknowledgements

My thanks to Gail Ashton for commissioning this title, and Fiona McCulloch as Series Co-Editor. Colleen Coalter and Laura Murray have been patient and encouraging editors at Continuum. I'm also delighted that a painting from Birmingham Museum and Art Gallery appears on the cover.

The School of Law, Social Sciences and Communications at the University of Wolverhampton, and Dean of School Judith Burnett, supported this book by awarding me a sabbatical. Florence Boos, Aidan Byrne, Mike Conley, Mark Jones, Martin Kratz, David Mabb, Rachel Mann and Jacqui Rowe all suggested references for Chapter 10.

I wrote some of this book at Gladstone's Library, Hawarden, North Wales, and there is no more conducive place to produce a Victorian writing project. A National Teaching Fellowship award (2011) facilitated these trips.

Special thanks go to Di Bishop, Jean Gilkison and Terry McKevitt. My favourite non-Victorian poet, Nicola Slee, has lived through this book's progress alongside me, and although I have yet to persuade her of the merits of Tennyson, she deserves my heartfelt love and thanks.

Permission to reproduce quotations has been kindly granted as follows:

Extracts from Arthur Symons courtesy of the Arthur Symons Literary Estate.

'A Ballad of London' courtesy of The Society of Authors as the Literary Representative of the Estate of Richard Le Gallienne.

'Blast' © by kind permission of the Wyndham Lewis Memorial Trust (a registered charity).

'The Dover Bitch' from *Collected Earlier Poems* by Anthony Hecht, copyright © 1990 by Anthony E. Hecht. Used by permission of Alfred A. Knopf, a division of Random House, Inc. Any third party use of this material, outside of this publication, is prohibited. Interested parties must apply directly to Random House, Inc. for permission.

'From Strugnell's *Rubáiyát*' from *Making Cocoa for Kingsley Amis* © 1986 by Wendy Cope. Reprinted by permission of Faber and Faber Ltd (excluding US rights). For US rights permission granted by United Agents on behalf of Wendy Cope.

'The Gentleman of Shalott' from *The Complete Poems 1927–1979* by Elizabeth Bishop. Copyright © 1979, 1983 by Alice Helen Methfessel. Reprinted by permission of Farrar, Straus and Giroux, LLC.

'Lady of Shalott Day' © Rachel Pantechnicon.

'Look We Have Coming to Dover!' from *Look We Have Coming to Dover!* © 2007 by Daljit Nagra. Reprinted by permission of Faber and Faber Ltd.

'To William Morris (1834-96)' by H.D. by permission of Pollinger Limited and New Directions.

PART ONE

Contexts

1

Social and cultural contexts

The varieties of Victorian poetry

Victorian poetry ranges from the soul-searchingly serious to the non-sensically comic; it encompasses Alfred Tennyson and Matthew Arnold *and* Edward Lear and Lewis Carroll. It is the protest poetry of Ebenezer Elliott's *Corn-Law Rhymes* (1831) and Thomas Hood's 'The Song of the Shirt' (1843). It is also the finely wrought jewel of Theodore Wratislaw's 'Orchids' (1896), in which 'bizarre sweet rhymes shall creep / Forth from my brain and slowly form and make / Sweet poems as a weaving spider spins' (16–18), and Mary F. Robinson's aesthetic sonnet 'Art and Life' (1891). It is awash with doubt, most famously in Tennyson's *In Memoriam* (*IM*) (1850), but also in the sardonic tone of Arthur Hugh Clough and much of Arnold: 'We mortal millions live *alone*' (4), stresses the unhappy speaker in 'To Marguerite' (1852) By contrast Gerard Manley Hopkins celebrates the diversity of a world still 'charged with the grandeur of God' ('God's Grandeur', 1918, 1).

Victorian poetry can be satiric, ready to mock the latest fads and fashions. Poet, dramatist and librettist William Gilbert teamed up with composer Arthur Sullivan to produce some of the most famous comic operas in the British tradition, including swipes at 'Professor of Aesthetics' Oscar Wilde and the cult of aestheticism in *Patience* (1881), and Tennyson's long poem *The Princess* (1847) and the 'Woman Question' in *Princess Ida* (1884). Pick up any edition of the humorous magazine *Punch* (started 1841) and light verse lampoons political, social and cultural subjects. Gilbert's *The 'Bab' Ballads: Much Sound and Little Sense* (1868, 1872) point to the

Victorian invention of nonsense poetry, which 'anticipate[s] and even rival[s] the extremes of modernist verbal experiment' (Cunningham, 2000, p. xliii). Edward Lear's 'The Owl and the Pussycat' (1871), 'The Jumblies' (1871) and 'The Dong with a Luminous Nose' (1877), and Lewis Carroll's 'Jabberwocky' (1872) have passed into our collective consciousness.

Some Victorian poetry is very long. This is an era that believes in the power of coherent narrative. Tennyson's *Idylls of the King* (1859–85) considers the state of the nation by retelling Arthurian legends; Elizabeth Barrett Browning's novel-in-verse *Aurora Leigh* (1856) explores the role of the woman poet; Robert Browning's *The Ring and the Book* (1868–9) recounts a seventeenth-century Roman murder told by the characters involved. Length is something that the reader of Victorian poetry must learn to appreciate as part of its design and seriousness of intent (see Roberts, 1999).

The shorter lyric is sensuously alive in the exultations of Christina Rossetti's 'A Birthday' – 'My heart is like a singing bird / Whose nest is in a watered shoot' (1861, 1–2) – and the lyric poem reasserts itself as the century progresses, so by the 1890s it is the most common form of poetic production. 'We are not sundered for we never met. / We only passed each other in the throng' (1–2) opens Olive Custance's 'Ideal' (1897), a momentary impression made by the 'flâneuring' of fin-de-siècle city life. Lear's limericks are only four lines, but can evoke more than their surface humour:

> There was an old man who screamed out
> Whenever they knocked him about;
> So they took off his boots, And fed him with fruits,
> And continued to knock him about.   (1872)

Half the length is Robert Browning's '[Rhyme for a Child Viewing a Naked Venus in a Painting of *The Judgement of Paris*]':

> He gazed and gazed and gazed and gazed,
> Amazed, amazed, amazed, amazed.   (wr. circa 1872; pub. 1925)

The title is practically longer than the poem (it has the same number of stressed beats, although they are irregular), but even such a short poem tells us important things about Victorian poetry. It flags up what is true of all British poetry of the period – that rhyme, repetition and metre are at the structural heart of what poetry is. The modernist poets who follow (though not the moderns) will take this assumption apart. Browning's two-liner also highlights what Carol Christ has termed the 'aesthetic of particularity' (Christ, 1975): the invention of photography and realist attention to detail in visual art mean that Victorian poetry starts to see in new ways.

Reform and protest

The poetry of the period registers the Victorians' attempts to come to terms with what Tennyson – inaccurately – praised as 'the ringing grooves of change' ('Locksley Hall' [1842], 182). In 1831 John Stuart Mill wrote a series of articles entitled 'The Spirit of the Age' which suggested that a self-consciousness about how the present was different to past eras was new, 'an idea essentially belonging to an age of change' (Mill, 1986, p. 228). Britain in the nineteenth century underwent irreversible societal transformation, due to the effects of the industrial revolution and a mass move of the populace from the country to the city. How this new kind of society should function, and the class-based antagonisms that arose as a result, are key issues in the 1830s to 1850s. The utilitarian principles of Jeremy Bentham and James Mill (John's father) – measuring the greatest good of the greatest number – underlie much thinking about societal organization in the early Victorian period, and posit the tension of the position of the individual in a fast-paced age of industrial growth and mechanization. Utilitarianism as a philosophy was also anti-feeling and based on rationality and exactitude. Bentham conceded that poetry could be useful, because it gave pleasure, but as poetry was a rarified pursuit it was no more valuable than the child's game of pushpin, enjoyed by many (Abrams, 1971, p. 301).

Several major Victorian commentators – Thomas Carlyle, John Stuart Mill and Matthew Arnold – critique what utilitarian and economic ideologies do to the individual, and suggest that poetry is one means to resist the dehumanization caused by such principles. Thus poetry is increasingly set apart from how society thinks about itself.

One of the first protests against materialism was Thomas Carlyle's 'Signs of the Times' (1829) in which he spoke of a 'Mechanical Age' distorting human consciousness. In Carlyle's *On Heroes, Hero-Worship and the Heroic in History* (1841), 'The Hero as Poet' is the third of six lectures. The need for heroes is urgent in Carlyle's writings, a desire for leaders in an era which seems not to have any fit for changing times. The Poet (capital P) is still a Hero (capital H) for Carlyle, and is akin to the subject of the second lecture – the prophet. The Carlylean poet also partakes of the topic of the first lecture – 'The Hero as Divinity'. Similarly, Mill published two essays on poetry in 1833: 'What is Poetry?' and 'The Two Kinds of Poetry'. Mill documents his 'discovery' of poetry retrospectively in his *Autobiography* (1873), describing how, in the mid-1820s, he experienced a depressive breakdown, and lost all faith in the principles which had hitherto guided his life, not least his father's utilitarianism. He realizes that 'the habit of analysis . . . wear[s] away the feelings' (Mill, 1989, p. 114) and it is through Wordsworth's poetry that he recovers 'a source of inward joy, of sympathetic and imaginative pleasure' (p. 121). In *Dipsychus and the Spirit* (1850) Clough questions what work has become in industrialized, factory-driven Britain. Behind all such critiques lies a moral concern about the mechanization of the individual human spirit:

> In all those crowded rooms of industry
> No individual soul has loftier leave
> Than fiddling with a piston or a valve.
> . . . .
> . . . We ask Action,
> And dream of arms and conflict; and string up
> All self devotion's muscles; and are set
> To fold up papers. To what end? We know not.
> Other folks do so: it is always done;
> And it is perhaps right. And we are paid for it.
> (Part Two, Scene 3, 121–3; 131–6)

The Victorian period is one of reform, with Reform Acts of 1832, 1867 and 1884 extending the male franchise. Chartism emerged in the later 1830s to press for the inclusion of working-class men in the political process (the 1839 Chartist Petition had over one million signatures), but was not successful. Chartist poets such as Thomas Cooper and Ernest Jones wrote powerful poems for the disenfranchised working man:

> We're low, we're low – we're very very low
> > Yet from our fingers glide
> The silken flow – and the robes that glow,
> > Round the limbs of the sons of pride.
>
> ('The Song of the Low' [1852], 31–4)

The emergence of the Socialist movement in the 1880s (the precursor to the British Labour Party) saw William Morris heavily involved. His political poems include *Chants for Socialists* (1884–5) and *The Pilgrims of Hope* (1885).

Protests against factory conditions include Caroline Bowles's *Tales of the Factories* (1833) and Caroline Norton's *A Voice from the Factories* (1836). Elizabeth Barrett Browning's 'The Cry of the Children' (1843) was a response to the Royal Commission Report on the Employment of Children in Trades and Manufactures (1842). The poem indicts a society that has put the making of profit above all other humanitarian considerations and uses a rhetorical, authoritative voice to highlight the plight of factory children. There is a repeated appeal to 'O my brothers', evoking anti-slave-trade speeches. 'The Cry of the Children' uses its emotional force to take on the entire British empire: '"How long," they say, "how long, O cruel nation, / Will you stand, to move the world, on a child's heart [?]"' (153–4). The poem helped the passage of the Ten Hours Amendment Bill (1844), limiting working hours for women and children.

Barrett Browning also wrote 'The Runaway Slave at Pilgrim Point' (1848), a dramatic monologue spoken by a black female slave fleeing from the white descendants of the original Pilgrim Fathers who first came to America from England. She does not have a name. Her identity is emphasized through repeated assertions of 'I am black, I am black' and she is a powerful emblem of female defiance. Shockingly the poem spends five stanzas describing the killing of her own child, a product of rape by white slave owners. The drama is heightened even more as the slave is pursued to the shore where there is nowhere else to go. Her final self-assertion is 'I am not mad: I am black' (218), and as the runaway slave is not prepared to submit to white mastery she chooses suicide by drowning.

Men and women

Industrialization can be regarded as one cause of the ideology of separate spheres which organizes gender roles in the Victorian period. The masculine, public world of work, action and economics, is set against the feminine, private world of the home, the domestic and emotion. This notion of the complementarity of the sexes is seen in John Ruskin's *Sesame and Lilies* (1864), and in Tennyson's *The Princess* (1847), which is a lengthy exploration of 'the Woman Question':

> Man for the field, and woman for the hearth;
> Man for the sword, and for the needle she;
> Man with the head, and woman with the heart;
> Man to command, and woman to obey;
> All else confusion.   (Part V: II, 437–41)

However, this is said by the *father* of the Prince who is the poem's leading male character. It is the view of an older generation. *The Princess* is all about trying to work out the 'confusion' of gender roles, as a cross-dressing Prince and his friends infiltrate a women-only university. The Victorian period saw women entering higher education for the first time and pressing for changes in the law which increased rights in marriage.

The pervasive ideal of woman being 'The Angel in the House' (from Coventry Patmore's poetical work of the same name celebrating marriage, 1854 and 1856) is not without dissenting voices. 'The altar, 'tis of death! For there are laid / The sacrifice of all youth's sweetest hopes', writes Letitia Landon (L.E.L.) in 'The Marriage Vow' (1873, 1–2). George Meredith dissects a marriage in *Modern Love* (1862), which opens with a husband and wife in their 'common bed' (I, 3) and the wife crying: 'Like sculptured effigies they might be seen / Upon their marriage-tomb, the sword between' (I, 14–15). Fifty jealous, brooding sonnets later it is far from clear they have a happy future.

As Isobel Armstrong suggests, 'Gender becomes a primary focus of anxiety and investigation in Victorian poetry which is unparalleled in its preoccupation with sexuality and what it is to love' (Armstrong, 1993, p. 7). 'How do I love thee? Let me count the ways . . .' opens Barrett Browning's most famous sonnet from *Sonnets from the Portuguese* (1850). Christina Rossetti writes a sonnet of sonnets in her sequence *Monna Innominata* (1881), in which a woman's voice takes on the male sonnet tradition of addressing the unattainable beloved. More controversially Dante Gabriel Rossetti was vilified for portraying a post-coital moment in 'Nuptial Sleep' (1870), and Swinburne uses the Hellenic to explore the sadomasochism of 'Laus Veneris' and 'Anactoria' and the gender ambiguity of 'Hermaphroditus' (1866). By the 1890s Arthur Symons is celebrating 'The chance romances of the streets' (4) in 'Stella Maris' (1894) and Ernest Dowson will praise 'Wine and women and song' in 'Villanelle of the Poet's Road' (1899).

The later nineteenth century witnessed a blurring of more rigid gender demarcations. Elaine Showalter reminds us that 'the words "feminism" and "homosexuality" first came into use, as New Women and male aesthetes redefined the meanings of femininity and masculinity' (Showalter, 1992, p. 3). May Kendall, Constance Naden, Rosamund Marriott Watson and Amy Levy all use poetry to explore women's changing sense of self at this time. The 1885 Labouchère Amendment became a blackmailer's charter for pursuing homosexual men and gained its highest profile scalp in Oscar Wilde's two-year imprisonment in 1895. Alfred Douglas, Wilde's lover, bequeathes us the phrase 'I am the love that dare not speak its name' (74) in the final line of 'Two Loves' (1894). Douglas also reclaims the word previously attached to any sexually transgressive woman: 'In Praise of Shame' (*The Chameleon*, 1894) turns shame into a queer code for homosexual desire (first attempted by Marc-André Raffalovich in *Tuberose and Meadowsweet* [1885]). Aunt and niece couple Katherine Bradley and Edith Cooper write as Michael Field, and their first joint volume, *Long Ago* (1889) is a response to Greek lyricist Sappho's fragments that make clear their lesbian overtones. A female desire for and joy in other women is celebrated in 'A Girl' (1893) and the sonnet 'Constancy': 'I love her with the seasons, with the winds, / As the stars worship, as anemones / Shudder in secret for the sun . . .' (1908, 1–3). But homoeroticism is not just a product of the naughty nineties. It is hard not to see it in that most central of Victorian poems, *In Memoriam*.

Gendering the poet

Gender is also at the heart of the problem that being a poet poses for both men and women at this time. The issue is that 'women *are* poetry. They live and inspire it but they do not write it, while other people – namely, men – have the privilege to do so' (Brown, 2000, p. 181; see also Mermin, 1995). The Victorian *poetess* is diminished by the very term. For men the dilemma is that poetry is associated with feeling, emotion, interiority and beauty – which the separation of gendered spheres regards as feminine. So the male poet is at constant risk of tipping over into a dangerous effeminacy.

Herbert Sussman notes how male poets had to negotiate 'a personal configuration of artistic manhood that was often at odds with the normative model of manliness in a bourgeois industrial society' (Sussman, 1995, p. 14). He suggests that 'male imaginative space is most often displaced in time, alternative masculinities situated in the past or in the future' (p. 44). Browning, Tennyson, Arnold, Morris and Swinburne all swerve into medieval, Renaissance and ancient classical contexts. Calls for a renewed, revitalized poetry in the period are often a rallying cry for the 'manly' poet to rise up (sic) and write the masculine epic (as opposed to lyric) poetry that the nation needs. Tennyson tries, in *Idylls of the King* (1859–85), but actually this work charts the *collapse* of male structural rule, as the Arthurian Round Table disintegrates. If the negative association of poetry with the feminine is something male poets must negotiate in the Victorian period, how much more is it an issue for the woman poet.

The Victorian woman poet

Sandra Gilbert and Susan Gubar's classic work *The Madwoman in the Attic* focuses on the anxiety of the woman author about her 'right to write' in an era which defines 'the pen [as] a metaphorical penis' (Gilbert and Gubar, 1979, p. 3). They remind us that it was *poetry* sent by Charlotte Brontë in 1837 to the then poet laureate Robert Southey that elicited his response 'Literature cannot be the business of a woman's life, and it ought not to be' (p. 545).

Victorian women's poetry can appear to mirror the ideological separation of men and women into differing spheres of influence through the construction of it as its own discrete tradition. Positively this involves the recognition of literary foremothers: Barrett Browning and Christina Rossetti praised Felicia Hemans and 'L.E.L.' before them just as Dora Greenwell, Bessie Rayner Parkes and Michael Field wrote tribute poems to Barrett Browning and Rossetti. If male poets are aware that the epic age of Homer has gone then the female equivalent is to honour the original Greek lyricist – Sappho. L.E.L., Caroline Norton, Christina Rossetti, William Sharp (Fiona Macleod) and Michael Field all do so (see Prins, 1999). More negatively, the separation of women poets into their own anthologies from the 1850s onwards constructs them as having a different history (Houston, 2002). Only with great difficulty are they allowed to inhabit the mainstream of just 'poetry'. Eight of ten volumes of Alfred Miles's *The Poets and Poetry of the Nineteenth Century* (1891–7) cover male poets chronologically up to those still living; volume seven alone features 'Joanna Baillie to Mathilde Blind'.

Victorian women poets also had to take on 'the pernicious assumption that women's poetry was always about personal experience and that its true subjects were home and the heart' (Leighton and Reynolds, 1995, p. xxviii). Women's lesser educational and societal opportunities account for why some Victorian women's poetry has differing concerns from men's. That said, many women poets engage fully with the issues of their day. Poetry is also one significant place where women 'talk back' to diminutive put downs of their writing and to the contradictions of how society positions them. Examples include Barrett Browning's *Aurora Leigh* (1856); Adelaide Procter's 'A Woman's Question', 'A Woman's Answer' and 'A Woman's Last Word' (1858); Rossetti's witty 'No, Thank You, John' and her wry response to brother Dante Gabriel, 'In an Artist's Studio' (1896); the 'ordinary, humble, downtrodden women' (Leighton and Reynolds, 1995, p. 418) who speak Augusta Webster's dramatic monologues;

George Eliot's 'Brother and Sister' sonnets (1874); Constance Naden's 'The Two Artists' and 'Love Versus Learning' (1881); May Probyn's monologue 'The Model' (1883); Mary E. Coleridge's spooky doppelgänger poem, 'The Other Side of a Mirror' (1896).

The fallen woman

W. R. Greg's essay 'Prostitution' (1850) suggested there were 50,000 prostitutes in London mid-century. Prostitution wasn't illegal, but it was regarded as *The Great Social Evil*, in the title of William Logan's 1871 book. The regulation of women's sexuality was a preoccupation of the Victorian period, and any woman who was sexually active outside of wedlock was potentially 'fallen'. While numerous journalistic and moral treatises condemn the fallen woman, poetry often treats her sympathetically. Thomas Hood's 'The Bridge of Sighs' (1844), evokes pity for the prostitute who has ended her life by jumping into the Thames:

> Mad from life's history,
> Glad to death's mystery,
> Swift to be hurl'd –
> Any where, any where
> Out of this world!   (67–71)

Social rehabilitation for the fallen woman – in literary depictions at least – is rare. The poem was influential, inspiring George Watts's painting *Found Drowned* (1848–60), which features a woman in cruciform position washed up under one of the arches of Waterloo Bridge.

William Morris uses a neo-medieval setting to bypass some of the problems of morality that beset Victorian realism in 'The Defence of Guenevere' (1858). The poem depicts Queen Guenevere being tried for adultery with Sir Launcelot by the knights of King Arthur's court. This is mostly a monologue, and enacts the content of the poem through its very form, as Guenevere's extended 'defence' of her love for Launcelot allows time for her lover to arrive and rescue her 'at good need' (295). Guenevere is that rarity in Victorian literature – a fallen woman who 'gets away with it' (unlike Guenevere in Tennyson's *Idylls of the King* [1859] or the adulterous woman in Augustus Egg's painted trilogy *Past and Present* [1858]). The cost, however, is written through the contortions of her body as she tries to defend her love and challenge the very paradigms of what truth means:

> But, knowing now that they would have her speak,
> She threw her wet hair backward from her brow,
> Her hand close to her mouth touching her cheek,
>
> As though she had had there a shameful blow . . .   (1–4)

Thomas Hardy's 'The Ruined Maid' (1901) also uses voices to enact the chance encounter between a 'raw country girl' (23) and the ruined maid of the title, who is a former friend. The poem's humour and pleasure hinge on the contrast between the old friend's memories of how "Melia' (1) used to dress, speak, live and look – 'You left us in tatters, without shoes or socks, / Tired of digging potatoes, and spudding up docks;' (5–6) – and the obvious contrast with how her 'ruin' has benefitted her materially: 'And now you've gay bracelets and bright feathers three!' (7).

There are also numerous poems about fallen women by women (see Chapters 5, 6 and 7). Less well known are Dora Greenwell's 'Christina' (1851), Rossetti's 'The Convent Threshold' (1858), Isa Blagden's 'The Story of Two Lives' (1864), Adelaide Procter's 'A Legend of Provence' (1877), Amy Levy's 'Magdalen' (1884), Mathilde Blind's 'The Message' (1891) and as a last gasp of Victorianism, Charlotte Mew's 'Madeleine in Church' (1916). As Angela Leighton comments, 'The fact that [these poems are] spoken in the first person . . . is an act of literary and social transgression' (Leighton and Reynolds, 1995, p. 276). There are repeating themes of renunciation, regret and repentance, but nevertheless the monologue form gives the fallen woman her own voice, and offers the woman poet a way of exploring a potentially taboo topic in a voice other than her own. The fallen woman speaker is almost always hedged round with the wider social and religious discourses which condemn her to think and speak of herself in a particular way, but the most successful of these poems engage with that tension as a dramatic possibility.

Doubt

Victorian poetry is a key place where debates and anxieties around shifting notions of belief are played out. The challenges to received understandings of Christian faith in the period come from two sources: advances in geological science and theological perspectives. Charles Lyell's *Principles of Geology* (1830–3) and Robert Chambers' *Vestiges of the Natural History of Creation* (1844) challenged biblical understandings of time. Charles Darwin's *On the Origin of Species* (1859) consolidated the notion of evolution through natural selection, whereby species mutate, develop and sometimes die out via a competitive process of the survival of the fittest. These ideas challenged the certainty of a creator God and the notion of divine will. Numerous poems engage with a post-Darwinian outlook, including Mathilde Blind's epic *The Ascent of Man* (1889), Mary F. Robinson's 'Darwinism' (1891), Constance Naden's witty 'Scientific Wooing' and 'Natural Selection' ('Evolutional Erotics', 1894), and May Kendall's satiric 'Lay of the Trilobite' (1885), 'Ballad of the Icthyosaurus' (1887), 'Woman's Future' (1887) and 'The Lower Life' (1887). In 'Égoisme à Deux' (1882) Louisa Bevington moves from the personal to the universal when she wonders how a love relationship fits into the huge vistas of time and absence of any presiding consciousness opened up by Darwinian evolution. The poem's four stanzas consist of questions but no answers:

> When the great universe hung nebulous
>   Betwixt the unprevented and the need,
> Was it forseen that you and I should be? –
>   Was it decreed?   (1–4)

Thomas Hardy's poetry is also located in that existentially angst-ridden place post-Darwin where the Christian God seems to have left the cosmos (see also Holmes, 2009).

Theological challenges to received understandings of the bible came from the German Higher Criticism of David Strauss's *The Life of Jesus* (1835–6) and Ludvig Feuerbach's *The Essence of Christianity* (1841). These works focussed on a human and historical approach to Christianity rather than emphasizing the divine. Benjamin Jowett's

Essays and Reviews (1860) brought higher critical principles to British theology. Arthur Hugh Clough was a tutor at Balliol College, Oxford, the same college as Jowett, but resigned in 1848 as he could no longer subscribe to the Church of England's Thirty-Nine articles. The disillusioned speaker of Clough's 'Easter Day. Naples, 1849' (1865) exorts the reader to 'Eat, drink, and play, and think that this is bliss! / There is no Heaven but this!' (77–8). The poem's repeated refrain is 'Christ is not risen, no, / He lies and moulders low; / Christ is not risen' (6–8). One of Clough's most well-known poems is his ten commandments rewrite for a materialistic Victorian age: 'Thou shalt have one God only; who / Would be at the expense of two? . . . Thou shalt not steal: an empty feat / When it's so lucrative to cheat' ('The Latest Decalogue', 1–2, 15–16).

The term 'agnostic' was coined in the 1860s by scientist Thomas Huxley, who argued that religious questions could only be answered by resorting to knowledge beyond reason. If scientific and theological developments could not be ignored, they left in their wake for some a terrible sense of having been abandoned by God, and a new consciousness of humanity's 'metaphysical isolation' (Wilson, 1999, p. 10). Arnold's 'Dover Beach' (1867) – one of Victorian poetry's most iconic poems – embodies this loss. The speaker and his love look out across the channel as the once 'full' 'sea of faith' (21, 22) now only offers its 'melancholy, long withdrawing roar' (25). The poem's answer to the implicit question of where does consolation lie in a world which 'Hath really neither joy, nor love, nor light, / Nor certitude, nor peace, nor help for pain' (33–4), is that it can only reside in individual personal relationships.

By the 1880s Arnold was a schools' inspector and influential commentator on matters of education and culture. Some of his most memorable statements on poetry concern its place within society, and these are inextricably linked to loss of faith in religious certainties. In 'The Study of Poetry' (1888) Arnold opens by quoting his own Introduction to *The English Poets* (1880):

> There is not a creed which is not shaken, not an accredited dogma which is not shown to be questionable, not a received tradition which does not threaten to dissolve . . . The strongest part of our religion today is its unconscious poetry.   (Arnold, 1987, p. 340)

Christianity will no longer save us, so poetry must fill the vacuum created: 'More and more mankind will discover that we have to turn to poetry to interpret life for us, to console us, to sustain us' (p. 340).

Faith

Despite the relationship between humanity and nature becoming increasingly troubled there is also still great praise and significant faith within Victorian poetry. 'And for all this, nature is never spent; / There lives the dearest freshness deep down things' (9–10) says Hopkins in 'God's Grandeur' (1918). Barely acknowledged in his own lifetime, Hopkins's extraordinary poetic language crackles with an exhilarating energy as he makes poetry embody the divine 'instress' he sees everywhere. This is also one of the great eras of hymn writing, and John Keble's *The Christian Year* (1827), a collection of devotional verses written for use alongside the Book of Common Prayer, was a bestseller. The Anglican piety of Christina Rossetti produced a significant body of poetic work, and 'A Christmas Carol' (1872) – better known as 'In the Bleak Midwinter' – is one of the best-known poems set to music.

In *English Poetesses* (1883) Eric Robertson suggested that 'faith is woman-like, doubt is man-like' (Leighton, 1992, p. 101). This is far too simple, but an emotional intensity does manifest itself in the religious poetry of Emily and Anne Brontë, Rossetti, Alice Meynell and Adelaide Procter. Emily Brontë's 'Death' and 'Remembrance' (1846), and oft-anthologized poems such as Rossetti's 'Song: (When I am dead, my dearest)', 'Up-Hill' and 'Remember' circle around an imaginative fascination with being out of this life. Armstrong suggests that 'religious poems are almost always concurrently poems about a woman's sexuality because the drama of religious devotion calls up adjacent emotions of sexual longing' (Armstrong and Bristow, 1996, pp. xxviii–xxix). This can be seen in the renunciation of Rossetti's 'After Death' in which the speaker says of her beloved as he leans over her newly dead body, 'He did not love me living; but once dead / He pitied me' (12–13). Alice Meynell's sonnet 'Renouncement' (1893) records her complicated love for the young priest who received her into the Catholic Church. Women are also among the many hymn writers of the period, as in Frances Havergal's classic lines of self-offering:

Take my love; my Lord, I pour
At Thy feet its treasure store.

Take myself, and I will be
Ever, *Only*, ALL for Thee.   (1884, 21–4)

Cecil Frances Humphreys (Mrs C. F. Alexander) wrote a primary-school staple in 'All Things Bright and Beautiful' (1848). These days school-children don't sing the notorious third verse: 'The rich man in his castle, / The poor man at his gate, / God made them, high or lowly, / And ordered their estate' (9–12). Francis Thompson's phantasmago-ric 'The Hound of Heaven' (1893) was still pursuing believers as the century drew to its close.

Empire

The background to all of the above is Britain's expansionist proj-ect of empire, which reaches its zenith in the Victorian period. In the 1879 edition of *The Angel in the House* Patmore explicitly links mid-Victorian attitudes to women with the colonization of empire:

A woman is a foreign land,
    Of which, though there he settle young,
A man will ne'er quite understand
    The customs, politics, and tongue.   (Book 2, Canto IX.2, 1–4)

The latter decades of the nineteenth century mark the high period of empire. Queen Victoria was proclaimed Empress of India in 1877, and the 'Scramble for Africa' of the 1880s saw numerous European powers carve up ownership of the continent. Victorian poetry of empire reaches its heights in the 1890s, particularly in the context of Queen Victoria's Diamond Jubilee of 1897, which was a whole-sale celebration of Britain's imperial might. Rudyard Kipling wrote poems such as 'The White Man's Burden' (1899) which appear to epitomize imperialist rhetoric, but he also ventriloquized the voices of working-class soldiers in more critical poems such as 'Tommy' (1890), 'Danny Deever' (1890) and 'The Widow at Windsor' (1890). Hardy also expressed sympathy for the soldier in 'Drummer Hodge' (1899). William Henley bequeathed influential lines when he asked 'What have I done for you, / England, my England?' ('Pro Rege Nostro', 1892, 1–2), and Henry Newbolt underscored the public-school, masculinist, sportsmanlike ethos of empire in the repeating last line of stanzas in 'Vitaï Lampada' (1897): 'Play up! play up! and play the game!'. Mrs Ernest Ames' illustrated children's book *An ABC, for Baby Patriots* (1899) helps explain how the ideology of empire carried on into successive generations:

> **E** is our Empire
>   Where the sun never sets;
> The larger we make it
>   The bigger it gets.   (17–20)

Reading

Bristow, Joseph, ed. (2000), *The Cambridge Companion to Victorian Poetry*. Cambridge: Cambridge University Press.

Cronin, Richard (2012), *Reading Victorian Poetry*. Chichester: Wiley-Blackwell.

Cronin, Richard, Alison Chapman and Antony H. Harrison, eds (2002), *A Companion to Victorian Poetry*. Oxford: Blackwell.

Cunningham, Valentine (2011), *Victorian Poetry Now: Poets, Poems, Poetics*. Chichester: Wiley-Blackwell.

Hughes, Linda K. (2010), *The Cambridge Introduction to Victorian Poetry*. Cambridge: Cambridge University Press.

Richards, Bernard (2001 [1988]), *English Poetry of the Victorian Period*. Harlow: Longman.

Research

- What is your favourite Victorian poem? How is it obviously Victorian? Why do you like it?

● Choose a poem that engages with contemporary Victorian social or political concerns. How does it do this differently from the way prose might?

● Focussing on one of the sections in this chapter, seek out at least two of the poems mentioned for discussion and comparison.

2

Literary contexts

The post-Romantics

Romanticism – a Victorian term to describe the sensibilities of art and poetry from the 1790s to 1820s – was a reaction against eighteenth-century neo-classicism. It was also a response to the start of the industrial revolution. As humanity becomes ever more dominated by machines, so the Romantic self stands against this inhuman power and celebrates the wonder-full force of nature. The Preface to the 1800 edition of Wordsworth and Coleridge's *Lyrical Ballads* (1798) set out Romantic poetry's concerns (a poetics). *Lyrical Ballads* aims to use 'a selection of language really used by men' (Gill, 1984, p. 597) as opposed to the stylized couplets of Pope and Dryden, and famously the Preface speaks of poetry as 'the spontaneous overflow of powerful feelings' (Gill, 1984, p. 611), making explicit the Romantic kinship of poetry and emotion.

In Romantic poetics and poetry that which is perceived is transformed through the imagination's power, and 'the imagination is God-like, in that its work parallels that of God in creation' (Watson, 1992, p. 12). In *The Prelude* Book VI (1850; wr. 1804–6) Wordsworth offers a great paean to the imagination: it is bound up with 'infinitude' (539), 'Effort, and expectation, and desire, / And something evermore about to be' (541–2). This brings us to the powerful sense of 'the poet' that the Romantics claimed for the one doing the perceiving or imagining. In *Lyrical Ballads'* Preface, the poet is 'endued with more lively sensibility . . . has a greater knowledge of human nature, and a more comprehensive soul, than are supposed to be common among mankind' (Gill, 1984, p. 603). Notably, this conception is gendered: the Romantic poet – the Blakean prophet, the Shelleyan revolutionary, the Coleridgean visionary, the Wordsworthian sage – *is* male. As noted in Chapter 1, this creates problems for women. The poet is special because he divines what Shelley calls the 'sword[s] of lightning' (Brett-Smith, 1947, p. 38) that are the elevated language and insights of poetry. 'Poets are the unacknowledged legislators of the world' (Brett-Smith, 1947, p. 59) claims Shelley in the triumphant final line of *A Defence of Poetry* (1840; wr.1821).

Shelley's *Defence* was a response to Thomas Love Peacock's *The Four Ages of Poetry* (1820), which dismissed some of Romanticism's assertions. Peacock refers to the current age of poetry as one of brass (rather than iron, gold and silver previously). The golden age of poetry – when Homer was writing – is long gone. Peacock sent Shelley a copy, and in the accompanying letter wrote 'there is no longer a poetical audience among the higher class of minds . . . moral, political, and physical science have entirely withdrawn from poetry the attention of all those whose attention is worth having' (Brett-Smith, 1947, p. xi). By the late 1820s four of the major male Romantic poets were dead – Keats (1821), Shelley (1822), Byron (1824) and Blake (1827) – and to a younger generation Wordsworth and Coleridge 'were burnt out stars' (Thomas, 1990, p. 1).

It is against this powerful backdrop of the status of poetry and the poet that poetry now defined as Victorian comes into being. In some Victorian poetry and poetics there is a sense of belatedness as poets and commentators make sense of what poetry can be and do in a fast-changing age that no longer seems to have any place for it. 'As civilization advances, poetry almost necessarily declines', wrote Thomas Macaulay in 1825 (Abrams, 1971, p. 306). Two decidedly 'post-Romantic' poems are Matthew Arnold's 'The Scholar Gypsy' (1853) and Elizabeth Barrett Browning's *Aurora Leigh* (1856). 'The Scholar-Gypsy' opens with a prose epigraph describing a story in *Glanvil's Vanity of Dogmatizing* (1661) about an Oxford student forced through poverty to leave his studies and live among a group of gypsies. He meets again two former student friends and tells them that the gypsies have 'a traditional kind of learning among them, and could do wonders by the power of imagination'. When he has fully learnt their secrets the scholar-gypsy says he will return to the sophisticated world to pass on his knowledge. In the first part of

the poem Arnold's speaker is in pursuit of the elusive scholar. When
the student friends appear the scholar-gypsy tells them 'the Gipsy
crew, / . . . had arts to rule as they desir'd / The workings of men's
brains; / And they can bind them to what thoughts they will' (44–8).
The gypsies' seeming magical powers stand as a metaphor for the
Romantic grasp of poetry's influence which the Victorian poet must
now do without. The scholar-gypsy clearly chooses a simpler way
of life, and the tone of the poem changes when the speaker 'wakes'
from enchantment with his quest and recognizes this is indeed a
story about the past. The remainder of the poem registers how it is
not possible to be a scholar-gypsy in the present because 'repeated
shocks, again, again, / Exhaust the energy of strongest souls' (144–5).
'Thou hadst *one* aim, *one* business, *one* desire' (152) says Arnold's
speaker enviously:

> O born in days when wits were fresh and clear,
>> And life ran gaily as the sparkling Thames;
>>> Before this strange disease of modern life,
>> With its sick hurry, its divided aims . . .   (201–4)

The language of contamination continues in the speaker's exhortation to the scholar-gypsy to 'fly our paths, our feverish contact fly! /
For strong the infection of our mental strife' (221–2).

If this is a melancholic post-Romantic response, a more posi-
tive claiming of the continued importance and power of the poet
features in *Aurora Leigh*, when Aurora encounters poetry for the
first time:

>   I write so
> Of the only truth-tellers now left to God,
> The only speakers of essential truth,
> Opposed to relative, comparative,
> And temporal truths . . .
>   . . . Ay, and while your common men
> Lay telegraphs, gauge railroads, reign, reap, dine,
> And dust the flaunty carpets of the world
> For kings to walk on, or our president,
> The poet suddenly will catch them up
> With his voice of thunder, – "This is my soul,

This is life, this word is being said in heaven,
Here's God down on us! what are you about?"
How all those workers start amid their work,
Look round, look up, and feel, a moment's space,
That carpet-dusting, though a pretty trade,
Is not the imperative labour after all.   (Bk I: 859–63, 69–80)

The poet's truth-telling is transcendent and prophetic, lifting the working man from his everyday labour into an encounter with something divine. Part of the passage's impact is because it is a female character who speaks and *Aurora Leigh* as a whole charts a woman's assertion of her right to the mantle of poet (see Chapter 5).

Early-to-mid-Victorian poetics

Victorian writing about poetry is different from the literary criticism or contemporary writing on poetry we might read today. Essays sometimes engaged in wide-ranging discussion about cultural and social matters before focussing on the poems. There is 'an almost complete absence of a specialized or technical critical vocabulary in Victorian reviewing' (Armstrong, 1972, p. 5), and attention to specific uses of 'poetic language' is relatively rare. Close reading or a form of practical criticism doesn't really happen.

Instead there is a distrust of that which seems strange, unfamiliar, or – in a word used of Browning's work – 'grotesque'. There is an appeal 'to the sympathies and affections of the reader, to those impulses which are aroused by the essentially "human" ties and feelings which we all can share' (Armstrong, 1972, p. 10). If the Romantics understood the perceiving mind of the poet as being like a lamp, illuminating and transforming what is seen, this is distrusted by some Victorian commentators who regard what the poetic mind does to the external world as distorting and falsifying. In the era of high realism art should be a mirror, not a lamp. As poetry clearly inhabits the realm of emotion for the Victorians, as it did for the Romantics, it is subjective, and this is increasingly pitted against the objective, the scientifically verifiable, the rational.

In 'The Philosophy of Poetry' (1835) Alexander Smith comments on how *'the fetters imposed by the verse'* (Bristow, 1987, p. 51) – the constraint of any rhythmic poetic form – means that the poet is granted a 'poetical license . . . to admit[ ] of verbal combinations, which, in prose, would seem far-fetched and affected' (p. 51). He also comments on features such as repetition, which 'add nothing whatever to the meaning; but . . . mak[e] words which are otherwise but the intimation of a fact, the expression of an *emotion* of exceeding depth and interest' (p. 45). This can be seen in Tennyson's poetry, where musical effects are harnessed to emotional meaning:

> Break, break, break,
> On thy cold gray stones, O Sea!
> And I would that my tongue could utter
> The thoughts that arise in me. (1842, 1–4)

Here the first line of the poem – repeated as the first line of the final stanza – is an example of such redundancy. The address to the waves to 'break' is given once, so why give it again, and again? Through the use of these three heavy single-stressed beats – which contrast with all other lines employing iambic (x /) or anapæstic (xx/) beats – a good deal of emotional weight is conveyed. This is a poem of grief, and it is not just the waves breaking.

George Henry Lewes suggested that 'Poetry must be emotive, it must be metrical – these are its conditions' (1842; Bristow, 1987, p. 57). But this focus on emotion and poetry as connected to interiority is problematic for commentators who want poetry to engage with the hurly-burly of politics, social division and the upheavals of Victorian modernity. The question of 'the competing demands made upon the poet either to participate in or retire from the turbulence of modern society' (Bristow, 2000, p. 4) is seen in responses to the early poetry of Tennyson.

Tennyson's Palaces of Art

Tennyson published *Poems, Chiefly Lyrical* (1830) aged 21, and to the reviewers here was something new. *Poems* (1833) followed. His reputation was sealed ten years later when *Poems* (1842) came out – the best of the earlier volumes with substantial revisions, including to 'The Lady of Shalott'. W. J. Fox offered one of the first reviews, in the Benthamite *Westminster Review* (1831), suggesting that poetry can be harnessed to utilitarian notions of progress: 'It would be a pity that poetry should be an exception to the great law of progression that obtains in human affairs . . . The machinery of a poem is not less susceptible of improvement than the machinery of a cotton-mill' (Jump, 1967, p. 21). Fox also sees scientific developments within poetry: 'metaphysical science has been a pioneer in poetry . . . in the analysis of particular states of mind' (p. 25). A brooding psychological intensity is characteristic of some of Tennyson's poetry (see 'Mariana' [1830] and *Maud* [1855]). However, Arthur Hallam's review (August, 1831) took the opposite view of poetry's purpose. Hallam allies Tennyson with Keats and Shelley as poets of 'sensation' and says that 'Whenever the mind of the artist suffers itself to be occupied . . . by any other predominant motive than the desire of beauty, the result is false art' (Jump, 1967, p. 35). Hallam celebrates the interiority in Tennyson's poetry as its own sign of the times:

> Hence the melancholy, which so evidently characterizes the spirit of modern poetry; hence that return of the mind upon itself, and the habit of seeking relief in idiosyncracies rather than community of interest. In the old times the poetic impulse went along with the general impulse of the nation; in these, it is a reaction against it . . .   (Jump, 1967, p. 41)

Although some of Tennyson's poetry will speak to issues of the day, Hallam argues it is not the poet's necessary role to do this. In 'the strange earnestness in [Tennyson's] worship of beauty' (p. 42) Hallam prefigures some of the central concerns of a later Victorian poetics influenced by aestheticism.

Three of Tennyson's 1832 poems explore the relationship of the artist–poet and art/poetry to society: 'The Lady of Shalott', 'The Palace of Art' and 'The Lotos Eaters'. Embowered in her tower, the Lady of Shalott is separated from Camelot which she can only look upon via the mirror's reflection. What does she do with the 'Shadows of the world' (48) she sees in her mirror? She turns them into the web of art. Is this an image of the Victorian artist–poet, whose very isolation from the fray means that (s)he is able to transform the impact of society into art? In 'The Palace of Art', a poem in implicit dialogue with Coleridge's 'Kubla Khan' (1816), the speaker writes of building his soul 'a lordly pleasure-house' (1) where 'My soul would live alone unto herself' (11). Into this fantastical palace are brought all the realms of heaven and earth and artistic greatness: the artist–soul can 'Commun[e] with herself' (181) in 'God-like isolation' (197) because she has everything she could ever need. However, in both poems this vision of the isolated artist goes horribly wrong: the attractions of a sparkly Lancelot prove catastrophically compelling for the Lady of Shalott, and in 'The Palace of Art' the soul is toppled from her lofty throne once the 'Uncertain shapes' (238) in the 'dark corners of her palace' (237) turn her dream home into a gothic castle of horrors. The Lady's leaving of her tower ultimately brings about her death, and the soul has to learn some humility in a lowly 'cottage in the vale' (291) before she is able to return to her 'beautifully built' (294) palace of art with others. The tension between the pleasures of aesthetic detachment and the necessity of societal engagement is also played out in 'The Lotos Eaters'. Far from home, Odysseus's men come to 'a land / In which it seemed always afternoon' (3–4) and the 'mild-eyed melancholy Lotos-eaters' (27) offer them a life of soporific ease. 'Is there confusion in the little isle?' they ask. 'Let what is broken so remain' (124–5). Odysseus's men choose to stay in the sensuous land of the Lotos, having 'had enough of action' (150), but again the refusal to engage with the chaos back home is far from as life-affirming as it might initially seem.

Arnold: Poetry and action

Aside from 'Dover Beach', Arnold may now be better remembered for what he said *about* poetry than for the poetry he wrote and his most well-known statements consolidate anxieties about 'a disabling focus upon the self' (Christ, 1984, p. 5). In the Preface to *Poems* (1853), Arnold writes negatively that 'the dialogue of the mind with itself has commenced' (Arnold, 1987, p. 41). This picks up on Hallam's line from 1831, but where Hallam valorizes a poetry of introspection Arnold says no enjoyment can come when 'suffering finds no vent in action' (p. 42). It is the poet's job to focus on 'what actions are the most excellent' (p. 43), whether present or past. The problem for Arnold, as seen in 'The Scholar-Gypsy', is that the modern age is so deficient. As it cannot supply the conditions for good poetry, the poet must take his or her cue from the ancient classics.

If the present only offers tawdry, insignificant 'actions', this implies that a poetry of the contemporary is doomed. However, a review of Arnold's volume by novelist Charles Kingsley, who features an aspiring working-class poet in his 1850 novel *Alton Locke*, enthusiastically suggested the opposite:

> There is poetry in Australian emigrations, Britannia-tubular bridges, Solent steam-reviews . . . it is to be longed and hoped for, that a poet may arise, even in our days, who will recover for us . . . our lost part in the harmony of spheres: but he must be a poet who can see the present; who understands the age in which he lives.   (Armstrong, 1972, p. 175)

The dramatic monologue

The Victorian period's most significant poetic development, the dramatic monologue, is 'a lyrical-dramatic-narrative hybrid. It absorbs an emotional expressiveness from lyrics, a speaker who is not the poet from drama, and elements of mimetic detail and retrospective structuring from narrative' (Slinn, 2002, pp. 80–1). The seemingly authentic lyric 'I' of Romantic poetry is looked askance at in the emergence of the monologue in the 1830s.

One tradition of its origins starts with Tennyson reading 'St. Simeon Stylites' to his friends in 1833 (pub. 1842) and Robert Browning publishing 'Porphyria's Lover' and 'Johannes Agricola in Meditation' in 1836. The name Browning gave to these two poems together in 1842 – 'Madhouse Cells' – emphasizes the idiosyncratic, disturbing or unhinged voices that speak some of his monologues. Tennyson's speakers are also often outsiders. In an 1852 advertisement for *Dramatic Lyrics* Browning said his poems were 'dramatic in principle, and so many utterances of so many imaginary persons, not mine' (Byron, 2003, p. 35). The distance between poet and speaker is important because it allows the monologue to explore material that it would be more difficult for the Victorian poet to consider if said in a lyric voice akin to their own. Joseph Bristow comments that

> With . . . the skill to proliferate the poet's identity into numerous personae, Victorian poetry managed to accommodate a startling range of themes . . . such as homicide, eroticism and irreligion . . . The persona – the dramatic voice – gave an extraordinary opportunity to the Victorian poet. (Bristow, 1987, p. 6)

Tennyson's *Maud*, for example (described as having one too many vowels in it), was the product of the now-fêted Poet Laureate. No one thought Tennyson was *quite* the same as his unstable poet-lover speaker. As Ekbert Faas notes, 'Deviance and abnormality would become a significant part of the tradition as the form developed; the poets moved into the darker areas of the mind, hovering, in the words of Browning's Bishop Blougram, "on the dangerous edge of things"' (Byron, 2003, p. 44).

In the twentieth century Browning was regarded as über Victorian monologist, hence the strong focus on the irony between the speaker's sense of self and the reader's alternative, 'superior' awareness of character. A more nuanced awareness of the form's variety shows the degree of irony to vary greatly. In the monologues of Augusta Webster and Swinburne, who are both concerned with matters of sexuality and social disapproval, there is less of a gap between the perspective of the speaker and the poet's likely view. It is also now recognized that women poets have as much to contribute to our understanding of the dramatic monologue as male ones, and a different account of the emergence of the form might cite Felicia Hemans' *Records of Women* (1828) and *Songs of the Affections* (1830), and poems by Letitia Landon. Monologues are also written by Dora Greenwell, D. G. Rossetti, Elizabeth Barrett Browning, William Morris, Amy Levy, John Davidson and Rudyard Kipling.

Poetry, the novel and marginality

The dramatic monologue offers psychological intrigue and explorations of consciousness as complex as in any character from a

Victorian novel. They situate their speakers in an implied context, and often suggest an auditor too. But by mid-century the novel has culturally moved centre stage in terms of addressing the complexities of Victorian society. 'There is no question', says Clough, in another review of Arnold, 'that people much prefer *Vanity Fair* and *Bleak House*' (Armstrong, 1972, p. 154). He continues: 'The modern novel is preferred to the modern poem, because we do here feel an attempt to include . . . phenomena which, if we forget on Sunday, we must remember on Monday . . . The novelist does try to build us a real house to be lived in' (p. 155). So poetry is pushed to the margins – socially, culturally, aesthetically. This might seem detrimental, but there are also possibilities in standing on Bishop Blougram's 'dangerous edge'. Victorian poetry does not function in the same way as realist prose, not least in terms of what can be said or represented. The fact that Victorian poetry is *poetry* – language marked by rhythm, stress and a lack of the transparency of realism – means it can explore more controversial subject matter that never overtly makes it into Victorian novels.

Poetry and the book arts

One way Victorian poetry explores its 'marginality' is via the specifics of publishing contexts, particular editions, book illustration and the growing interest in the aesthetic book:

> Victorian publishers like Routledge and Moxon at mid-century, and John Lane at the *fin de siècle*, capitalized on the fact that a book's 'prettiness' could be used to attract consumers for whom an illustrated volume of poetry, displayed in a lady's drawing room or an aesthete's private library, provided a visible sign of the owner's cultivation and refinement.   (Kooistra, 2002, p. 392)

The development of the illustrated book in the Victorian period is due to technological developments in printing and processes for reproducing images (e.g. wood engraving in the 1830s and 1840s). The 1857 Moxon edition of Tennyson's poems featured illustrations by numerous painters of the day, including the Pre-Raphaelites Dante

Gabriel Rossetti, William Holman Hunt and John Millais. Tennyson did not like having his poems illustrated, raising the potential 'tussle for power' between word and image, poet and illustrator, in any illustrated edition. Other Victorian poets actively embrace the publication of their poems alongside images, and the 'idea of the total book' as synthesis of word, image and book design (McGann, in Kooistra, 2010, p. 5). 'The Lady of Shalott' is the Victorian period's most visually responded to poem, with over fifty images produced by the end of the century, and many more since (see Chapter 10).

Poets connected to the Pre-Raphaelites are central to poetry and the book arts. The definition of a 'Pre-Raphaelite poem' has been the subject of much discussion, both in the mid-Victorian period and since. Often the term is used loosely to refer to poets in some way associated with the Pre-Raphaelite painters – Morris, D. G. Rossetti, Christina Rossetti, Swinburne – but these four are widely diverse in style. 'Pre-Raphaelite' was of course a designation for visual art before it was connected with poetry and the short-lived Pre-Raphaelite periodical *The Germ* (1850) featured images alongside text. Morris's *The Defence of Guenevere* volume (1858) occasioned the first attempts of reviewers to apply the term to poetry, often with a sense of bafflement (see Faulkner, 1973). From the outset Morris was concerned with the presentational aspects of his poems' publication, and in the 1860s he wished to publish the neo-Chaucerian *The Earthly Paradise* (1868–70) as an illustrated project with woodcut images by Edward Burne-Jones. The printing technology of the time prevented its realization. In the meantime Morris produced one-off exquisite calligraphic manuscripts, such as his own *A Book of Verse* (1870) and Edward Fitzgerald's *The Rubáiyát of Omar Khayyám* (1873), to ensure composite control over the production of his poetic works. It is not until 1891, and the establishment of his own Kelmscott Press, that Morris can create his 'ideal book' as illustrated, designed artefact, producing editions of his own poems and others he admired.

Christina Rossetti's *Goblin Market and Other Poems* (1862) and *The Prince's Progress and Other Poems* (1866), with illustrations by her brother, signal her importance to discussions of Victorian illustrated poetry. The 1893 edition of *Goblin Market,* with its gold embossed art nouveau cover and illustrations by Laurence Housman, make it one of the 1890s' most notable poetry books. By the late 1860s Dante

Gabriel was successful as a painter, but the work-a-day commissions that were his bread and butter meant less to him than the publication of his first volume of poems in 1870 (see Fredeman, 2004). Jerome McGann has argued that Dante Gabriel's commitment to the book arts was a lifelong interest, evident in his own editions (McGann, 2010), and many of Rossetti's paintings have accompanying sonnets either in the painting itself, or etched into their frames.

The Christmas gift book market and illustrated annuals such as *The Keepsake* also brought word and image together. The early-nineteenth-century annual 'helped to establish and profession-alize the work of women writers, particularly the poets' (Leighton and Reynolds, 1995, p. xxvi). Gender also plays its part in the 'relations' of word and image in illustrated books as in so many other areas of Victorian poetry. A particularly unpleasant sonnet by Wordsworth in 1846 regards poetry as regressing 'From manhood – back to childhood' due to the 'vile abuse of pictured page!' (Kooistra, 2002, p. 395). In the latter part of the century, when the aesthetic book-as-designed-art-object is all the rage, and photogravure tech-niques have improved quality again, 'one of the consequences of the pairing of picture and poem for an increasingly specialized mar-ket of gift buyers and collectors . . . was to associate verse with a commodity either feminine or effete' (p. 415). Some of the most notable editions of 1890s poetry are designed by Charles Ricketts and Charles Shannon, who established a more fin-de-siècle version of the Kelmscott Press in the Vale Press of 1896. Oscar Wilde took 220 unbound copies of his 1881 *Poems* to the most savvy 1890s' pub-lisher of them all – John Lane at The Bodley Head. With a cover and title page by Ricketts and each copy numbered and signed by Wilde, Lane saw a marketing opportunity exquisitely fit for the year of 1892. Ricketts also illustrated and designed an edition of Wilde's decadent poem *The Sphinx* (1894), with its long sinuous lines matched by the elongated contours of Ricketts' striking images and decoration (see Frankel, 2000). John Gray's *Silverpoints* (1893), also designed by Ricketts (with more margin than text), prompted Wilde's friend Ada Leverson to suggest that Oscar should 'publish a book *all* margin; full of beautiful unwritten thoughts' (Kooistra, 1995, p. 130). By the end of the century, then, the busier printed pages of earlier volumes and publishing contexts had given way to 'poetry now appear[ing] in its own space' (Kooistra, 2010, p. 4).

Later Victorian poetics

As Carol Christ has noted, 'Most writing on Victorian poetics sees a sharp distinction between poetry in the first and second halves of the period' (Christ, 2002, p. 11), with the Pre-Raphaelite poets, and responses to them, marking the break. Richard Buchanan wrote an anonymous review of Dante Gabriel Rossetti's *Poems* (1870) in 1871 and found their sensuous sexuality 'simply nasty' (Bristow, 1987, p. 145). Rossetti wrote a defensive response, and these articles became the 'Fleshly School' controversy. Similarly Swinburne's *Poems and Ballads* (1866) provoked almost universal vitriol for their eroticism, sadomasochism, Republican tendencies and paganism. Publisher Edward Moxon withdrew the volume. Up for a literary fight, Swinburne replied to his critics with 'Notes on Poems and Reviews' (1866), and homed in on the key wider issue:

> It is this: whether or not the first and last requisite of art is to give no offence . . . Who has not heard it asked . . . whether this book or that can be read aloud by her mother to a young girl? . . . Never till now, and nowhere but in England, could so monstrous an absurdity rear for one moment its deformed and eyeless head.   (Bristow, 1987, p. 158)

Swinburne's concern is with censorship and moral assumptions being brought to bear on what can and can't be said in art and literature. He continues this argument in an 1868 essay on William Blake, using one of the later nineteenth century's most notable artistic phrases: 'Handmaid of religion, exponent of duty, servant of fact, pioneer of morality, she [art] cannot in any way become . . . Art for art's sake first of all, and afterwards we may suppose all the rest shall be added to her' (Small, 1979, p. 5). *L'art pour l'art* – the idea that the artist's duty is to formal excellence over 'content' or any ethical factors – becomes a rallying cry for the aesthetes and decadents of the later Victorian period. The phrase was first used by Théophile Gautier in the preface to *Mademoiselle de Maupin* (1835), but Swinburne's usage helped popularize it this side of the channel.

The phrase is also used by Walter Pater, the critic who 'provide[s] the philosophical framework for the poetics of the century's final decades' (Christ, 2002, p. 16). Pater's 1868 review of Morris's poems occasions a number of phrases which will etch themselves like fire into the consciousness of a new generation of younger, mostly male, poets of the fin de siècle. The intensity that Pater perceives in Morris widens into an aesthetic philosophy of life:

> Not the fruit of experience but experience itself is the end. A counted number of pulses only is given to us of a variegated, dramatic life . . . How can we pass most swiftly from point to point, and be present always at the focus where the greatest number of vital forces unite in their purest energy?
>
>   To burn always with this hard gem-like flame, to maintain this ecstasy, is success in life. Failure is to form habits . . .
>
> (Faulkner, 1973, p. 91)

This becomes the (in)famous conclusion to Pater's *The Renaissance* (1873). In its preface Pater takes on critical responses to poetry that are striving for an objective, universally-agreed response to art and subversively suggests that the subjective is the most important thing in aesthetic discrimination. Morris and Rossetti have helped shape this view. Pater wrote favourably in *Appreciations* (1889) that 'One seems to hear there [in Rossetti] a really new kind of poetic utterance, with effects which have nothing like them' (Bristow, 1987, p. 171).

Elsewhere in *The Renaissance* Pater writes that '*All art constantly aspires towards the condition of music*' (Pater, 1986, p. 86). The sensuous effects of sound are actively pursued by Swinburne and Wilde: 'Before his gilded galiot ran naked vine-wreathed corybants, / And lines of swaying elephants knelt down to draw his chariot' ('The Sphinx', 1894, 99–100). Hear also the divine soundscapes of Hopkins's theological aestheticism:

> I caught this morning morning's minion, king –
> > dom of daylight's dauphin, dapple-dawn-drawn Falcon, in his riding
> > Of the rolling level underneath him steady air, and striding
> High there . . .   ('The Windhover', 1918, 1–4)

The lyric reasserts itself at the fin de siècle – the subjective 'I' singing its beautifully crafted song. Gautier's *Émaux et Camées* (1852, enamels and cameos) embodies this sense of the later-nineteenth-century lyric as a finely wrought shimmering jewel.

French poets Paul Verlaine, Arthur Rimbaud, Stéphane Mallarmé and Charles Baudelaire also influence 1890s poets. Bad boy Charlie had *Les Fleurs du Mal* (1866, the flowers of evil) banned nine years before Swinburne achieved the same, and his strong conception of 'the artist' as a way of life and his urban outsider poetics had a significant impact on fin-de-siècle poetry. In 1859 he wrote 'le beau est toujours bizarre' (the beautiful is always strange) and this is an apt sentiment for when 'art for art's sake' modulates into the 'experience for experience's sake' of decadence. These French poets also lurk in the background of the myth of the 1890s poet:

> . . . a shadowy man who hovered for a few crucial years on the edge
> of literary notice before sinking into a fog of despair, dissipation, and
> death. Typically the life was as brief as the fleeting lyric cries that
> accompanied its descent into obscurity.   (McCormack, 2005, p. 47)

In one sense this *is* a myth, as numerous poets associated with the 1890s lived well into the twentieth century (Symons, Gray, Le Gallienne, Yeats). Ernest Dowson and Lionel Johnson, however, did die young, and what could be more 'fin de siècle' than the ennui-laden nihilism of Enoch Soames, who sold his soul to the devil. It is remarkable that his volumes *Negations* and *Fungoids* are not better known (see Beerbohm, 1997; Lasner, 1999).

By the 1890s poetry was becoming more diverse, and as well as no single poet dominating the landscape, 'there was a dizzying array of poetic movements, genres, types and coteries'. This worked to the benefit of women as 'women poets were publishing in such great numbers . . . that there is no longer a polarity between a "women's tradition" and a mainstream' (Thain, 2007, p. 224). While aestheticism and decadence can appear predicated on a homoerotic gender politics that is misogynistic, women poets were well aware of the artistic and literary trends of their day and both participated in and critiqued them (see Schaffer and Psomiades, 1999; Rodensky, 2006). Michael Field spend an entire volume gazing at paintings in *Sight and Song* (1892); Rosamund Marriott Watson, Olive Custance and Dollie Radford all had poems published in the decadent movement's

notorious periodical, *The Yellow Book*; and Anglo-Indian Sarojini
Naidu was first published in *The Savoy*.

The end of the century also sees a revival of interest in the ballad.
These include Kipling's *Barrack-Room Ballads* (1892), A. E. Housman's
A Shropshire Lad (1896), and *The Ballad of Reading Gaol* (1898) – by
C.3.3., the most (in)famous prisoner of the century – with its distinctive six-line stanzas. Amy Levy's 'Ballade of an Omnibus' (1889)
and 'A Ballad of Religion and Marriage' (1915) use the French ballade
form, which had also been used by Andrew Lang in his aesthetically
titled *Ballades in Blue China* (1880). John Davidson's 'Ballad of a Nun
(1894), Aubrey Beardsley's 'Ballad of a Barber (1896) and Richard Le
Gallienne's 'A Ballad of London' make the ballad form decadent:

> Ah, London! London! our delight,
> Great flower that opens up at night,
> Great City of the Midnight Sun,
> Whose day begins when day is done.   (1895, 1–4)

The ballad is also Thomas Hardy's favourite form, underpinning the
variety and innovation of stanza constructions across his significant
poetic œuvre.

The ballad, as Wordsworth knew when naming *Lyrical Ballads*, is
'of the people', as opposed to the courtly conceits of blank verse and
the sonnet (Easthope, 1983). Whether poetry as a whole remains 'of
the people' by the end of the nineteenth century is a moot point. If
Romanticism was a reaction against industrialization, one hundred
years on poets are embracing the city and finding the beautiful in gas
lights and prostitutes. Wilde, in his contempt for the Philistine public
that Arnold was so keen to educate, is perfectly content that poetry
has become marginal. In a reversal of the alarum cries of 'whither
poetry?' in the earlier nineteenth century, the fact that the public
want increasingly little to do with it is now part of its greatness:

> In England, the arts that have escaped best are the arts in which
> the public take no interest. Poetry is an instance of what I mean.
> We have been able to have fine poetry in England because the
> public do not read it, and consequently do not influence it.
>
> ('The Soul of Man Under Socialism' [1891], 1966, p. 1091)

Reading

Bristow, Joseph, ed. (1987), *The Victorian Poet: Poetics and Persona*.
London: Croom Helm.
Byron, Glennis (2003), *Dramatic Monologue*. London: Routledge.
Christ, Carol T. (2002), 'Introduction: Victorian Poetics', in *A Companion
to Victorian Poetry*, ed. Cronin, Chapman and Harrison, pp. 1–21.
Oxford: Blackwell.
Kooistra, Lorraine Janzen (2002), 'Poetry and Illustration', in *A
Companion to Victorian Poetry*, ed. Cronin, Chapman and Harrison,
pp. 392–418. Oxford: Blackwell.
Thain, Marion (2007), 'Poetry', in *The Cambridge Companion to the Fin
de Siècle*, ed. Gail Marshall, pp. 223–40. Cambridge: Cambridge
University Press.

Research

● Read some Victorian reviews of any Victorian poet. How do they
talk about poetry? What do they consider significant, or new, in
the poet's work?

● Compare Arnold's 'The Scholar Gypsy' with *Aurora Leigh*, Book 1,
lines 854–80. Discuss their differing responses to modernity.

● How do 'The Lady of Shalott', 'The Palace of Art' and 'The Lotos
Eaters' dramatize the relationship between artist–poet and
society?

● Using a good research library, look at a first edition of a Victorian
volume of poems. Consider it *as a book*. Is it illustrated? What
do you notice about the binding and cover? How is the poetry
laid out inside? Is this different to poetry volumes now?

● Using an anthology such as Thain and Thornton (1997) or
Rodensky (2006) choose a poem and argue for how it embodies
a fin-de-siècle poetics.

PART TWO

Texts

Introduction: Reading Victorian poetry

Part Two offers a number of poems for more detailed discussion. My choices have been determined by an awareness that some poems are more likely to be taught than others, a desire to represent both male and female poets, and personal affection for certain poets and poems. My aim is to offer a 'way in' to these poems to readers who are perhaps not familiar with them, providing a range of contexts through which they can be better understood. I also offer my own readings, which I hope will stimulate readers to attempt their own.

Victorian literature is often taught with much attention paid to embedding texts in their social, cultural and historical contexts. While this is absolutely necessary there is also a danger, particularly with poetry, of this approach: '[m]ost students, faced with a . . . poem, spontaneously come up with what is commonly known as "content analysis"', but '[w]hat gets left out is the *literariness* of the work' (Eagleton, 2007, pp. 2–3). A poem's ostensible 'meaning' cannot be separated out from its specific formal features that contribute to the very creation of that meaning. So in approaching Victorian poems that are thematically 'about', say, faith and doubt, or the fallen woman, the best readings will be attentive to how metre, word choice, rhythm, stanza form, imagery and other poetic, literary features support the reading being made.

Victorian metres and rhythms

The lingering sense (for some) that a poem is not a 'proper poem' unless it is written in a regular rhythm in a formal pattern, probably comes from the after-memory of Victorian poetry. For the Victorians a poem simply wasn't a poem unless it was written with an underlying poetic metre. Often – though not always – poems also rhymed. Within a British context there was no such thing as free verse at this time. Prosody is the name given to the study of a particular poem's use of stress and metre, and it helps us to 'pick out moments where a poem seems especially affecting, surprising or impassioned' (Williams, 2009, p. 133). Often poems are saying interesting things at points where the natural rhythms of speech are in tension with the stress pattern of an underlying poetic metre. I sometimes discuss metrical patterning and use a simple notation of (x) to mark off-beats and (/) to mark stressed beats in a poetic line. I have also glossed any poetic terms that may be unfamiliar, such as the names of the most common poetic metres. I encourage readers to engage with the prosody of the Victorian poems they read. This will enhance your enjoyment as well as make you appreciate their skill. To understand fully how difficult or easy it is to write well in metrical verse readers are encouraged to have a go themselves (see Fry [2005] and Attridge [1995]).

3

Alfred Tennyson, *In Memoriam* (1850)

In the first week of October 1833, Tennyson received a letter saying his beloved friend, Arthur Henry Hallam, had died in Vienna of a burst blood vessel in the brain. Hallam was 22. Alfred and Arthur had met at Cambridge, and Hallam's death has been described as 'unquestionably the central event of Tennyson's life' (Perry, 2005, p. 17). The same month Tennyson started composing sections of the poem that would take seventeen years to complete, and which would cement his reputation as *the* poet of his generation. *In Memoriam* (hereafter *IM*) is one of the Victorian period's greatest poems. It is an intimately personal poem, with its heart 'l[ying] in grief at a human loss' (Ormond, 1993, p. 102), and also a public poem, which captures the immensity of a people bereaved in the face of modernity. *IM* is as much about coping with the death of religious certainty as it is about Tennyson finding a way to go on after Hallam's death. It also dramatizes some of the issues about gender and sexuality that are intrinsic to thinking about Victorian poetry itself.

'What Hope is Here for Modern Rhyme?' (LXXVII. 1): *In Memoriam* and form

IM is made up of 133 numbered sections, topped and tailed by a Prologue and Epilogue. Clearly the poem is rooted in an event in Tennyson's life, but we should beware of reading the sections as adding up to a cumulative autobiographical whole (see Sinfield, 1986, p. 124). Tennyson himself said

> . . . this is a poem, *not* an actual biography . . . The sections were written at many different places . . . I did not write them with any view of weaving them into a whole, or for publication, until I found that I had written so many.   (Tennyson, 1897, vol. 1, p. 304)

Nonetheless *IM* does have a certain structure, and Tennyson described how the poem fell into nine broad sections: I–VIII, IX–XX, XXI–XXVII, XXVIII–XLIX, L–LVIII, LIX–LXXI, LXXII–XCVIII, XCIX–CIII, CIV–CXXXI. There is a sense of the movement of time, marked by successive Christmases appearing in the poem in the years following Hallam's death. Leonée Ormond suggests that emotionally the poem moves 'from shattering, chilling, grief to the affirmation of a continuing evolution towards human perfection' (Ormond, 1993, p. 102). *IM* is thus part of the literary tradition of elegy. Just as the sonnet tries to cross the gap between lover and beloved, so the elegy aims to bridge the impossible gap between mourner and mourned. *IM* can also be linked to the sonnet: in that it is an extended sequence of short lyric poems it is akin to sonnet sequences, where the whole adds up to more than the individual parts. *IM*'s distinctive ABBA stanza form has also been linked to the sonnet: 'it is a Petrarchan sonnet that never reaches the turn of the sestet, and the poem as a whole a sequence of disappointed sonnets: there is a ubiquitous feeling of incompleteness' (Perry, 2005, p. 136). Formally *IM* tells us it is about loss and grief, *and* love and desire.

Let's take a closer look at that stanza form:

XII

Lo, as a dove when up she springs
 To bear through Heaven a tale of woe,
 Some dolorous message knit below
The wild pulsation of her wings;

Like her I go; I cannot stay;
 I leave this mortal ark behind,
 A weight of nerves without a mind,
And leave the cliffs, and haste away

O'er ocean-mirrors rounded large,
  And reach the glow of southern skies,
  And see the sails at distance rise,
And linger weeping on the marge,

And saying: 'Comes he thus, my friend?
  Is this the end of all my care?'
  And circle moaning in the air:
'Is this the end? Is this the end?'

And forward dart again, and play
  About the prow, and back return
  To where the body sits, and learn
That I have been an hour away.   (Ricks, 1989, p. 357)

This is section XII in full, where the speaker contemplates the bringing back of Hallam's body from Europe by sea. This is one of the
most grief-stricken sections: the anticipation of the ship's arrival is
unbearable ('I cannot stay'). The speaker imagines himself out of the
present moment of waiting into the (literal) flight of fancy of likening
himself to a dove which can fly away to the 'glow of southern skies'
(evoking Alfred and Arthur's summer holiday trip to Cauteretz in the
Pyrenees in 1830) and which can 'linger weeping on the marge' at a
safer emotional distance. But just as stanza three suggests an eas-
ing of the pain, the next stanza brings us back to it in the bird circling
the boat as though returning to an open wound. Note the rhetorically
distraught questions in stanza four. Is this the end of what? Of all life?
Of love? There is also a kind of death-wish in this lyric (a melancholic
tone is part of Tennyson's poems more widely): in the extremities
of grief the world is emptied of value because the loved one is no
longer a part of it. There is a desire to 'leave this mortal ark behind'.
Tennyson's dove evokes the dove in Genesis 8.8–9, which is sent
from the ark to find dry land and at first cannot. There is nothing
here but treading water in waves of grief, and the 'forward . . . back'
movement of stanza five evokes the relentless, queasy movement
of being so carried.

The end of section XII jolts the speaker and reader out of
imaginative reverie. To emphasize this we do not just go 'back'
or 'return', but we 'back return' (18) to the visceral pain of 'where

the body sits' (19). The speaker almost awakes as from a dream to 'learn / That I have been an hour away' from his standing watch on the cliffs. Arnold's 'Dover Beach' is another poem which imagines a speaker looking out anxiously across the channel, and the same implicit nationalistic tendencies are here as Hallam, cut off in his youthful prime, was destined for a career of influence. At the end we are taken back to the beginning, or even prior to the beginning, and the previous section's 'calm despair' (XI. 16). Section XI repeats the word 'calm' eleven times, sometimes twice in the same line. This massive over-repetition starts to empty the word of all meaning: it becomes a mantra through which the speaker tries to 'calm' himself in the face of the emotional tumult of having to greet the oncoming ship. This move to return us to the beginning is characteristic of *IM* as a whole and is embodied in the very stanza form itself with its ABBA rhyme scheme. The very final word of each stanza is needed to complete the rhyme but at the same time it takes us back to line one, prior to lines two and three which have attempted to take us somewhere new, both in thought and sound patterns: 'the poem repeatedly announces its imminent purpose to move on, but finds itself lingering' (Perry, 2005, p. 135).

In Memoriam as elegy

Tennyson attempts to find a form in words to express his deep personal grief, but this most private of expressions is also very public. The elegy as literary genre goes back to Theocritus's *Idylls* (3 BC); significant English examples are the funeral elegies of Spenser, Donne and Milton's 'Lycidas' (1638). *IM* is now part of the history and development of the poetic elegy and elegy itself is 'a self-conscious performance in which the elegist asserts his [sic] own poetic skill and becomes part of a pre-existent tradition or lineage of similarly skilled poets' (Kennedy, 2007, p. 13). *IM* is highly self-conscious about the paucity of language to represent grief. When the speaker says it is 'The lesser griefs that may be said' (XX. 1) the profoundest grief seems beyond articulation. He sees qualities in Hallam now he is dead that he did not see when alive – 'A likeness, hardly seen before' (LXXIV. 3) – but 'what I see I leave unsaid' (LXXIV. 10).

In *IM* 'the elegist starts to watch himself elegizing' (Kennedy, 2005, p. 59) and in section XXI the speaker imagines himself as the pastoral elegist of classical tradition:

> I sing to him that rests below,
>   And, since the grasses round me wave,
>   I take the grasses of the grave,
> And make them pipes whereon to blow.   (XXI. 1–4)

The elegist imagines the questioning of such 'private sorrow' (14) in an era 'When more and more the people throng / The chairs and thrones of civil power?' (15–16) and 'When Science reaches forth her arms . . . and charms / Her secret from the latest moon?' (18–20). His response is consistent with the sense of the Victorian poet asserting the value of what they do amidst conditions that may, on the surface, seem antithetical to poetry: 'I do but sing because I must' (23).

Later, in section LVII, our speaker suggests that 'my work will fail' (8), connecting it through rhyme to the final enigmatic line of the previous section, 'Behind the veil, behind the veil' (LVI. 28). Answers to many of the existential, philosophical and religious questions that the poem poses are indeed shrouded from view, but one thing is certain: *IM* didn't fail. The critics were broadly very favourable and 8000 copies had been printed by Christmas 1850. Tennyson had written a poem which captivated the nation, and despite its wide frames of reference its 'broad meaning was readily comprehensible' (Ormond, 1993, p. 105). It was also the poem that clinched the Poet Laureateship (Wordsworth died just as *IM* was published). Later Tennyson would recount an extraordinary dream about the Laureateship offer:

> The night before I was asked to take the Laureateship, which was offered to me through Prince Albert's liking for my *IM*, I dreamed that he came to me and kissed me on the cheek. I said, in my dream, 'Very kind, but very German.' In the morning the letter about the Laureateship was brought to me and laid upon my bed.   (Ricks, 1989, pp. 219–20)

Tennyson's unconscious was obviously an interesting place. After the death of Victoria's beloved Albert in 1861 he wrote to console the

Queen, saying how, after Hallam's death, he 'suffered what seemed to me to shatter all my life so that I desired to die rather than to live' (Ricks, 1989, p. 109). Queen Victoria told him that 'next to the Bible *IM* is my comfort' (Sinfield, 1986, p. 1). His first published poem as Poet Laureate, 'To the Queen' (1851), was written using the *IM* stanza.

The job of the traditional (pre-twentieth-century) elegy is ultimately to console: 'the endpoint of any adequate response to loss is successfully persuading yourself . . . that the diminished world is still worth enduring' (Perry, 2005, p. 128). In part this is determined by the Christian notion of resurrection: Christ overcomes death and there is new life. But the question of whether there is any such thing as life after death in a recognizably Christian sense is one of many with which the poem grapples. Towards the end of *IM* there are some signs that the speaker is able to turn from the past to the present again. CXV opens 'Now fades the last long streak of snow, / Now burgeons every maze of quick[set thorn]' (1–2) and this section repeats 'now' five times, and echoes it through 'flowering' (3), 'drowned' (7), 'down' (10) and numerous vowel half rhymes. Tennyson is a master of matching landscape or setting to emotional mood (see 'Mariana') and here 'in my breast / Spring wakens too' (17–18). The following section suggests he is even able to imagine the future: 'Yet less of sorrow lives in me / . . . Than some strong bond which is to be' (CXVI. 13, 16). But there is no obvious final assertion of Christian resurrection; rather '*Love* is and was my Lord and King' (CXXVI. 1 and 5, emphasis mine). Hallam is imagined as here and not here, a 'dear spirit, happy star' (CXXVII. 18) who 'Oe'rlook'st the tumult from afar' (19) and who has been dispersed in quasi-mystical fashion into all of nature: 'Behold I dream a dream of good, / And mingle all the world with thee' (CXXIX. 11–12). In the penultimate section the speaker asserts that Hallam is now 'mixed with God and Nature' (CXXX. 11) and thus 'I have thee still' (14). In this way *IM* does elegy's traditional work of denying that death is death, if not quite being able to assert the Christian theological way of doing this. The final section addresses the 'living will that shalt endure' (CXXXI. 1), which one might think is an abstract address to God, but Tennyson glossed it as 'Free-will, the higher and enduring part of man' (Tennyson, 1897, vol. 1, p. 319). What ultimately matters in this elegy is that it can imagine Hallam as never lost.

Honest doubt

IM does have moments of more conventional Christian hope, particularly when Christmas is evoked, as if the speaker feels he *should* be a bit more cheerful at this time of year. Sections XXVIII–XX refer to the first, most painful Christmas after Hallam's death. The festivities remind the family that 'A merry song we sang with him / Last year' (XXX. 15–16), emphasizing his absence, and that they are all 'making vain pretence / Of gladness' (XXX. 6–7). The hope of 'Ring[ing] in the Christ that is to be' (CVI. 32) is much later the final, almost exultant line of the wonderful 'Ring out, wild bells, to the wild sky' (1). It is one of the most hopeful sections in the entire poem, with the final line of each stanza for once pointing forward, ringing in the good and true.

But '*wild* bells . . . *wild* sky'. There is 'evidence of a willed hope shaping the poem's structure that exceeds the emotional truthfulness of its component parts' (Perry, 2005, p. 130). On such occasions *IM* feels like a forced rictus grin on a sad face. Jahan Ramazani has suggested that 'the modern elegist tends not to achieve but to resist consolation, not to override but to sustain anger, not to heal but to reopen the wounds of loss' (Ramazani, 1994, p. xi). His concern is with Hardy onwards, but *IM* is on the way to this state. The most lingering emotional sense in the poem is an awareness of its immense struggle to do or be anything other than overwhelmed with grief and loss.

It is *IM*'s hesitancy and uncertainty, its inability to be consoled, that make this personal account of abandonment resonate with much larger losses. For the Victorians also experience themselves as abandoned by the 'great[est] Love-object' – God (Wilson, 1999, p. 13). Scientific advances in the nineteenth century concerning geology and evolutionary understandings of the planet and natural world started to call into question the Genesis biblical account of creation and the concept of a loving, anthropocentrically concerned God. T. S. Eliot memorably wrote '[*IM*] is not religious because of the quality of its faith, but because of the quality of its doubt. Its faith is a poor thing, but its doubt is a very intense experience' (Eliot, 1951, p. 336). *IM*'s Prologue, composed in 1849 close to publication, starts with one of those assertions of 'willed hope':

> Strong Son of God, immortal Love,
>   Whom we, that have not seen thy face,
>   By faith, and faith alone, embrace,
> Believing where we cannot prove;
>
> Thine are these orbs of light and shade;
>   Thou madest Life in man and brute;
>   Thou madest Death; and lo, thy foot
> Is on the skull which thou hast made.
>
> Thou wilt not leave us in the dust:
>   Thou madest man, he knows not why,
>   he thinks he was not made to die;
> And thou hast made him: thou art just.   (Prologue 1–12)

There is *almost* an affirmation of a benevolent creator Christ/God here, but even by line three 'faith alone' must stand in for what cannot be seen. We must 'Believ[e] where we cannot prove' and 'think' (but not be sure) we were 'not made to die'. It is repeatedly stated that God has 'madest' man, but amidst all this creedal-sounding assertion, man 'knows not why'. The Prologue continues with such equally ambivalent lines as 'Thou *seemest* human and divine' (13) and 'We have *but* faith: we cannot know' (21; emphasis mine). *IM* is very hesitant about religious certainty. Its doubt makes it modern, *and* of its time.

After the overwhelming grief of the early sections the poem considers whether there is still some kind of afterlife or resurrection of the body. 'Behold a man raised up by Christ!' exclaims the speaker about Lazarus (XXXI. 13), but only to wonder whether Lazarus had wanted to hear those left behind grieving for him. In XXXIII the speaker admonishes himself not to upset his sister's simpler faith even though he is aware of how his 'faith has centre everywhere, / Nor cares to fix itself to form' (3–4). This is immediately followed by:

My own dim life should teach me this,
    That life shall live for evermore,
    Else earth is darkness at the core,
And dust and ashes all that is.   (XXXIV. 1–4)

Note the 'should'. The speaker wants to believe there is an afterlife because the alternative in lines three and four is too awful, and contains no possibility of reunion with Hallam. Tennyson apparently did maintain some belief in an afterlife; in an 1870 conversation he said:

. . . he did not require argumentative proof of a future life, and referred me to *IM*. He had nothing further to say; and, although his faith was not stated dogmatically in that poem, every one could see that he believed in the survival of the individual.   (Page, 1983, pp. 182–3)

Section XCVI echoes XXXIII in having the speaker address someone – possibly Emily Sellwood, Tennyson's soon-to-be wife – who tells him 'doubt is Devil-born' (4). The speaker's response is 'I know not' (5), but what he did know was one who was 'In many a subtle question versed' (6). Hallam's ability to wrestle with nuance is favoured over Emily's desire for certainty and this leads to one of *IM*'s most famous assertions: 'There lives more faith in honest doubt, / Believe me, than in half the creeds' (11–12). *IM* was not Tennyson's first poem to grapple with issues of belief and doubt: 'Supposed Confessions of a Second-Rate Sensitive Mind Not In Unity With Itself' (1830) and 'The Two Voices' (1842, begun 1833) rehearse themes that *IM* makes its own. But hesitation, vacillation and doubt are *IM*'s raison d'être in terms of both subject matter and structure. Its 'doctrinal indecisiveness' (Perry, 2005, p. 139) lies behind its 'honest incapacity, as though registering in the disappointment of genre the spirit of an unpropitious age' (p. 140).

'Nature, Red in Tooth and Claw' (LVI. 15)

IM recognizes that whatever faith it can manage is conceived in the face of scientific advances which pose challenges to what was once unquestioningly believed. The Prologue hints at this when it seems to pray 'Let knowledge grow from more to more, / But more of reverence in us dwell' (25–6). By the time of *IM* the ideas found in William Paley's *Natural Theology* (1802), which argued that evidence for the existence of God could be found in the design of the natural world, were being challenged by geological science. When Tennyson was an undergraduate the Cambridge Apostles debating society discussed the question 'Is an intelligible First Cause deducible from the phenomena of the Universe?' Tennyson voted no (Tennyson, 1897, vol. 1, p. 44). Late in *IM* there is an implicit rejection of Paley: 'I found Him not in world or sun, / Or eagle's wing, or insect's eye' (CXXIV. 5–6).

The stanzas most quoted in relation to the development of evolutionary thought in the 1830s and 1840s are LIV–LVI. Charles Lyell's *Principles of Geology* (1830–3) – 'one of the seminal scientific works of the nineteenth century' (Wilson, 1999, p. 160) – was read by Tennyson in late 1836. Based on the evidence of fossils, Lyell suggested that whole species have gone extinct over huge vistas of time, far outreaching biblical understandings of history and the creation of the world. Robert Chambers' *Vestiges of the Natural History of Creation* (1844) also prepared the way for Darwin by suggesting that one species has evolved from another. Evolutionary thought ultimately suggests that 'Nature' is an impersonal, unfeeling force, and human beings are caught up in its massive processes of change just like any other creature. The response to this in *IM* is overwhelming religious doubt:

> Are God and Nature then at strife,
>   That Nature lends such evil dreams?
>   So careful of the type she seems,
> So careless of the single life;
>
> That I, considering everywhere
>   Her secret meaning in her deeds,
>   And finding that of fifty seeds
> She often brings but one to bear,
>
> I falter where I firmly trod,
>   And falling with my weight of cares

Upon the great world's altar-stairs
That slope through darkness up to God,

I stretch lame hands of faith, and grope,
    And gather dust and chaff, and call
    To what I feel is Lord of all,
And faintly trust the larger hope.   (LV. 5–20)

Tennyson registers through these last two stanzas the emotional sense of bereavement such scientific advances had on the Victorians. What will happen to those 'Who loved, who suffered countless ills' (LVI. 17)? To all human endeavour? Will they too end up as Paley's fossils, 'sealed within the iron hills?' (20). The only answer is 'Behind the veil, behind the veil' (28).

'My Lost Desire' (CXXIX. I)

As *IM* heads towards its end there is still much uncertainty about the absent God made paradoxically manifest through recent scientific discoveries. 'God' is 'invoke[d]' in terms increasingly abstract, piled up in hesitant lists:

That which we dare invoke to bless;
    Our dearest faith; our ghastliest doubt;
    He, They, One, All; within, without;
The Power in darkness whom we guess . . .   (CXXIV. 1–4)

Five sections later another quasi-divine figure is evoked in a stanza that seems to echo this one. But where the one referred to above we have to *dare* invoke, this one is

Known and unknown; human divine;
    Sweet human hand and lips and eye;
    Dear heavenly friend that canst not die,
Mine, mine, for ever, ever mine.   (CXXIX. 5–8)

This 'Strange friend' (9) appears to be a Christ-infused Hallam, the one whom the speaker finds a way to keep with him always at the end of *IM*. Kennedy writes of the 'nineteenth-century elegy as a history of elegy's public work being overrun by desire' (Kennedy, 2007, p. 64) and nowhere is this more so than in *IM*.

The suggestion earlier of *IM* as made up of incomplete, fractured sonnets seems entirely appropriate, for this is surely also one of the Victorian period's great love poems. Alan Sinfield said of *IM* that 'Always there is the danger of an unattributable excess of sexual implication' (Sinfield, 1986, p. 146). Making this point in 1986 was more taboo than it is now, and Sinfield's provocative proposal was that the scandal is more in the refusal of some readers to see the force of the poem's same-sex desire than in any suggestion that Tennyson might have been gay. He deliberately 'avoid[s] suppressing the intimacy of the poem' by 'writing "Arthur" where commentators normally put "Hallam"' (Sinfield, 1986, p. 117).

The question of how to deal with a poem in which the speaker says 'I cannot love thee as I ought' (LII. I) is one with which Tennyson's biographers and critics have had to grapple. Christopher Ricks responds at some length to his own assertion that 'Anyone who believes that Tennyson's feelings for Hallam were not homosexual should try to say why' (Ricks, 1989, p. 206). Ormond comments on Tennyson falling in love with Rosa Barings and then Emily Sellwood in the mid-1830s: 'Before the "discovery" of Rosa, the biographical material provided few indications that Tennyson was sexually attracted towards women. That he had some kind of empathy with them is beyond doubt' (Ormond, 1993, p. 67). *IM* ends in a long Epilogue imagining the marriage of Tennyson's youngest sister Cecilia to his friend Edmund Lushington with Alfred as the father figure giving her away. This Epilogue could be read as a transmutation of his own forthcoming marriage – in June 1850 – but Ormond also notes the relatively low-key nature of their wedding (Tennyson didn't want it reported in the press) and that although '*IM* extols the importance of the marriage bond . . . the hasty, secretive way in which the wedding was arranged suggests deep insecurities on Tennyson's part' (p. 107). On their honeymoon they made a pilgrimage to Hallam's grave. Seamus Perry's fine book on Tennyson, with a particular focus on his use of language, sets itself against 'much recently ideologically minded criticism', which looks for 'the wholly unmagical things that the poetry leaves unsaid, or only barely says, or unwittingly lets slip' (Perry, 2005, p. 5). Perry has critics such as Sinfield and Eve Kosofsky Sedgwick in his sights here and his hesitancy over such readings is perhaps because he feels they are rather too crudely single-minded in what they are looking to 'reveal', at the expense of an attentiveness to the complex nuances of Tennyson's language. Sedgwick's influential *Between Men: English Literature and Male Homosocial Desire* (1985) features Tennyson's *The Princess* (1847) as part of its argument that 'the European [literary] canon as it exists is already [a male homosocial] canon, and most so when it is most heterosexual' (Sedgwick, 1985, p. 17), and it is more than possible to have a Sedgwick-fest with *IM* in relation to her triangular understanding of male homosocial desire as cemented through the exchange of women. Hallam was engaged to Tennyson's sister, who was also, interestingly, an Emily. In LXXXIV the speaker imagines the life Hallam might have had: 'For now the day was drawing on, / When thou shouldst link thy life with one / Of mine own house' (10–12).

In a BBC radio programme on Tennyson former Poet Laureate Andrew Motion said: 'I wouldn't quite want to say that he's a gay poet, but I wouldn't mind if somebody did' (*Searching for Alfred*, 2009), and to regard *IM* as haunted by the unspoken is not just to connect that to the intensity of grief. What makes *IM* so full of desire is that it *does* find a language – indeed, is part of creating a language – for 'The wish too strong for words to name' (XCIII. 14), in a line which pre-echoes Alfred Douglas's famous 'the Love that dare not speak its name' ('Two Loves', 1894). One of the most compelling readings of *IM*'s same-sex desire is Christopher Craft's, which uses the speaker's plea to Hallam to 'Descend, and touch, and enter' (XCIII. 13), and this line directly precedes 'The wish too strong for words to name'. Craft notes that 'a certain anxiety attends the reading of *IM* and always has' (Craft, 1994, p. 47) and he argues for how the language of homosexual desire which the poem creates as a mid-nineteenth-century discourse of male same-sex love is 'here constituted only elegiacally' (p. 51). The poem's struggle – and failure – to let go of grieving for Hallam and to move on mimics the impossibility of speaking of same-sex love as in any way present. Words cannot name it at this historical moment in time. The nearest we get are moments of 'trance' (XCV. 43) or dream sequences (which inevitably pass) in which 'all at once it seemed at last / The living soul [of Hallam] was flashed on mine' (XCV. 35–6).

Miss Alfred Tennyson

Craft also notes a 'fear of the unhinged gender within Tennyson's poetic voice' (p. 47). From the outset Tennyson faced imputations of effeminacy in relation to his writing of an emotionally sensuous lyric poetry. He frequently inhabits the voices of female characters in his earlier poems. As discussed in Chapter 1 the male Victorian poet is often figured as dangerously close to the feminine:

> . . . whether a male poet directly impersonates a woman or not, the experience of a wavering sexual identity, of feminization, may inevitably occur when he explores the terrain of lyrical emotion – a terrain characterized by the interconnected emotions of loss, pain, passion and desire.   (Maxwell, 1997, p. 82)

Kennedy also notes that lamentation can appear unmanly: 'male weeping is closely associated with anxieties about losing and saving face. So male mourning is necessarily associated with self-absorption, with self-watchfulness under the gaze of others' (Kennedy, 2007, p. 28). We might here think of the lyric 'Tears, idle tears' in *The Princess*, and if it wasn't written in five-line iambic pentameter stanzas it wouldn't be out of place in *IM*. As noted earlier, *IM* is also a very watery poem. When Hallam's body is brought back across water the speaker says he is 'filled with tears that cannot fall' (XIX, II); instead the lyric itself weeps, containing the waters of the Danube, the Severn, the Wye, wave[s] (4), 'salt sea-water' (6), tide[s] (13), 'wave[s] again' (13). 'I brim', says the speaker, 'with sorrow drowning song' (12). If *IM* involves Tennyson starting to watch himself elegizing then this self-consciousness also extends to the performance of masculinity on offer.

   IM was initially published anonymously, and although Tennyson's authorship was soon ascertained this did not stop a couple of early reviews thinking it was by 'a female hand' (*Literary Gazette*, June 1850; Ricks, 1989, p. 208). An unsigned review in *Tait's Edinburgh*

Magazine (August 1850) writes with amusement of how 'the literal tendencies of [a] critic discovered a female hand, and hailed the rising of a new poetical star in a widow's cap' (Dixon Hunt, 1970, p. 72). *The Times* reviewer, under no illusions about the writer, regarded the 'second defect' of the poem as its 'tone of . . . amatory tenderness. Surely this is a strange manner of address to a man' (28 November 1851; Dixon Hunt, 1970, p. 104). Ormond comments on hostile critics apportioning Tennyson's lyrical abilities as a poet to 'Miss Alfred Tennyson' (Ormond, 1993, p. 99).

So from the outset the poem caused confusion among its readers about the appropriateness of its gendered tone. Today we might be surprised that critics did not comment even more on the poem's ways of writing its love for Hallam which seem to twenty-first-century readers far more suffused with sexual longing. One of the most common ways that the speaker imagines his relation to Hallam in the poem is as his spouse, or – more accurately – his widow or (less often) widower. The highly charged line 'Descend, and touch, and enter' was actually a substitute for the manuscript line 'Stoop soul and touch me: wed me' (Ricks, 2007, p. 436). There are many further examples of this: Hallam is 'My Arthur, whom I shall not see / Till all my widowed race be run' (IX. 17–18); 'Tears of the widower' (XIII. I) fall as the speaker imagines 'Her place is empty' (4) in the bed beside him; he wishes he 'Could . . . forget the widowed hour' (XL.I); 'My spirit loved and loves him yet, / Like some poor girl whose heart is set / On one whose rank exceeds her own' (LX. 2–4); LXXXV speaks of 'My heart, though widowed' (113). As already mentioned, the poem also concludes with what Craft refers to as a 'thumpingly symbolic heterosexual marriage that so famously and unconvincingly closes . . . the elegy' (Craft, 1994, p. 63). By this point we know who it is that Tennyson would have liked to marry. There is no sanctioned 'available' language to talk of love between men, so Tennyson 'destabilizes the heterosocial contract by using familiar male-female analogues to represent male-male desire' (Morgan, 2000, p. 221).

IM offers us 'the provocative idea of male femininity' (Sinfield, 1986, p. 143). There is no doubt that Hallam was Tennyson's ideal man – 'manhood fused with female grace' (CIX. 17) – and that as well as loving him Tennyson used the poem to imagine how literally world-changing he might have become had he lived: 'A lever to uplift the earth / And roll it in another course' (CXIII. 15–16). Hyperbolic, perhaps, but we have already seen how Hallam is ultimately dispersed throughout all Nature. 'Disseminated Hallam inseminates everything' says Craft (p. 61). Hallam is not lost, but 'turned to something strange' (XLI. 5) – into one of the Victorian period's most astonishing, complex, queerest poems.

Reading

Kennedy, David (2007), *Elegy*. London: Routledge.
Perry, Seamus (2005), *Alfred Tennyson*. Tavistock: Northcote House.
Ricks, Christopher (1989), *Tennyson*. Basingstoke: Macmillan.
Sinfield, Alan (1986), *Alfred Tennyson*. Oxford: Basil Blackwell.

Research

- *IM* repays careful, attentive close reading. Take any one of its sections and offer your own detailed analysis, paying attention to the use of language and form.

- Consider *IM*'s relationship to contemporary scientific and theological debates and challenges to Christian belief.

- Discuss the suggestion that *IM* is as much a love poem as an elegy.

4

Robert Browning's monologues

In 1856 George Eliot reviewed Robert Browning's new volume *Men and Women*:

> Let [the reader] expect no drowsy passivity in reading Browning. Here he will find no conventionality, no melodious commonplace, but freshness, originality, sometimes eccentricity of expression; no didactic laying-out of a subject, but dramatic indication, which requires the reader to trace by his own mental activity the underground stream of thought that jets out in elliptical and pithy verse. To read Browning he must exert himself . . .
>
> (Bristow, 1991, p. 33)

Browning is responsible for innovations in the use of voice, style and form that have had lasting influences on how poetry developed into the twentieth century, and created poems where what is *not* said becomes as important as what is. Eliot's appreciative review was unusual for Browning in 1856, who produced much of the poetry for which he is best remembered in relative obscurity. As Eliot says, Browning's poetry requires the reader to *work*, and almost from the outset it was labelled 'difficult' (particularly *Sordello* [1840]). Walter Bagehot notoriously described his work as 'grotesque' in the *National Review* (1864). It was not until *The Ring and the Book* (1868–9) that Browning truly became an acclaimed and popular poet, although at more than 21,000 lines we might well think *this* work is going to be difficult. A not-insignificant number of Browning's poems, including many of his dramatic monologues, are substantial in length and run into hundreds of lines.

This may sound like I am trying to put readers off. Far from it. Browning's poetry is full of energy, surprise, colloquial vigour, a frank enjoyment of sexuality and a revelling in God's world. His characters are every bit as unforgettable as any from your favourite Victorian novel. What more metrical energy can a reader want than 'The Pied Piper of Hamelin' (1842):

> Rats!
> They fought the dogs and killed the cats,
>   And bit the babies in the cradles,
> And ate the cheeses out of the vats,
>   And licked the soup from the cooks' own ladles,
> Split open the kegs of salted sprats,
> Made nests inside men's Sunday hats,
> And even spoiled the women's chats
>   By drowning their speaking
>   With shrieking and squeaking
> In fifty different sharps and flats.   (10–20)

The length of many Browning poems suggests that his intention was to immerse readers in the vivid worlds he creates. He also repays being read in a good edition with helpful notes, as many of his most well-known poems are engaged in a creative dialogue with historical fact – particularly the history of the Italian Renaissance and its art.

Browning and the dramatic monologue

Browning (born 1812), like Tennyson, is a post-Romantic poet. He was aware that the powerful impact of the male Romantic poets was no longer in its first flush. He wrote scathingly of Wordsworth in 'The Lost Leader' (1845), 'Just for a handful of silver he left us, / Just for a riband to stick in his coat' (1–2). Wordsworth was Poet Laureate by this time, but many thought he had lost his earlier visionary power. Browning's hero was Shelley, and as a teenager he embraced his atheism, vegetarianism and radicalism. While none of these youthful enthusiasms lasted, Shelley's powerful notion of poetry as partaking of the divine in 'A Defence of Poetry' inspired the young Browning's own poetic vocation. In 1852 Browning paid tribute in 'An Essay on Shelley', and made a distinction between the subjective and objective poet. Browning's first published poem, *Pauline* (1833), also shows Shelley's influence.

In 1835 Browning met actor-manager William Macready. This was an important friendship as Browning's developing poetic style 'grew out of the same passionate interests in acting and actors and live theatre' (Hawlin, 2002, p. 17). The speaking voice in Browning's monologues – its stops and starts, exclamations, hesitancies and pauses for effect – employs *dramatic* techniques, and this is the term Browning used to name his volumes: *Dramatic Lyrics* (1842), *Dramatic Romances and Lyrics* (1845), and following on from *Men and Women* (1855), *Dramatis Personae* (1864). The latter, of course, is Latin for the list of characters in a play. Famously Browning wrote in the advertisement for *Dramatic Lyrics* that his poems are 'dramatic in principle, and so many utterances of so many imaginary persons, not mine' (Byron, 2003, p. 35). He was aware of the need to state this and was marking out his difference from the more subjective use of the lyric 'I' by his Romantic predecessors. Stefan Hawlin emphasizes the dramatic monologue's clear borrowings from drama when he describes it as 'a play that ha[s] shrunk to one speech by one character. From that one speech we can infer a wider dramatic situation' (Hawlin, 2002, p. 61).

'Porphyria's Lover'

Initially simply 'Porphyria' when it appeared in the *Monthly Repository* (1836), this and 'Johannes Agricola in Meditation' are often regarded as the first two Victorian dramatic monologues to be published. Tennyson was independently developing his own version of the monologue at the same time but his most famous monologues

('St. Simeon Stylites', 'Ulysses' and 'Tithonus' were not published until 1842). When the two poems were published in *Dramatic Lyrics* in 1842 they appeared under the joint heading of 'Madhouse Cells'.

The poem opens with a brief sense of setting: 'The sullen wind was soon awake . . . And did its worst to vex the lake: / I listened with heart fit to break' (2, 4–5). The opening five lines are all we get of this before attention turns to the contrast that Porphyria's entering the cottage makes: 'She shut out the cold and the storm' (7). What is notable in the next few lines is the passivity of the speaker:

> . . . she sat down by my side
> And called me. When no voice replied,
> She put my arm about her waist,
> And made her smooth white shoulder bare,
> And all her yellow hair displaced,
> And, stooping, made my cheek lie there,
> And spread, o'er all, her yellow hair . . .   (14–20)

Not just one of these things happened, but this, and this, *and* this . . . There is clearly a sexual charge too. The speaker notes that Porphyria 'Murmur[s] how she loved me' (21), but the poem's next few words can be interpreted in different ways, and exemplify how the compression of the monologue, and what it leaves out, is all important. Porphyria's lover says that 'she [is or was] / Too weak' (21–2) to 'give herself to me for ever' (25), but the missing verb surely matters. If she *is* too weak, then what is going on in their close physical proximity? If she *was* too weak, but now has set her 'struggling passion free / From pride' (23–4) then the suggestion is that this is a longed-for moment of sexual intimacy.

The poem pivots around the speaker's recognition of this moment: 'I looked up at her eyes / Happy and proud; at last I knew / Porphyria worshipped me' (31–3). When the next words are 'surprise / Made my heart swell' (33–4) we may deduce this is not the only organ gaining in size. Browning has been described as 'the great early celebrant of heterosexual desire' (Sussman, 1995, p. 73) and love is one of his major preoccupations. Browning's treatment of love relationships is 'very different from the way in which they generally feature in nineteenth-century novels, where . . . they are treated within a wider social context. [Browning's] poems are focused on the *inside* of relationships, their privacy' (Hawlin, 2002, p. 96). Thus 'Porphyria's Lover' can be read as a more disturbing version of the 'good minute' ('Two in the Campagna', 50) theme in Browning's poetry; that is, the question of how to hold on to 'the precious moment of closeness between two human beings that does not endure' (O'Gorman, 2004, p. 204). In 'By the Fire-Side' (1855) the speaker imagines that in 'life's November' (5) he will recollect places visited with his beloved and this leads him to eulogize the 'moment, one and infinite!' (181) of shared communion between lovers. In 'Two in the Campagna' (1855) the desire of the speaker to hold on to the thought he 'touche[s]' (6) amidst the spring countryside outside Rome becomes a celebration of unfettered sexuality: 'Such life here . . . Such primal naked forms of flowers, / Such letting nature have her way' (26, 28–9). There is an intense desire to be at one with the beloved – 'I would that you were all to me, / You that are just so much, no more' (36–7) – but this is impossible: 'No. I yearn upward, touch you close, / Then stand away' (46–7). Before he knows it 'the good minute goes' (50). Being human is to live with the 'wound' (40) of this inability to sustain connection and an awareness of 'Infinite passion, and the pain / Of finite hearts that yearn' (59–60).

Returning to 'Porphyria's Lover', the speaker's 'moment she was mine, mine, fair' (36) is captured in an altogether more unsettling way when the sentence ends 'I wound / Three times her little throat around, / And strangled her' (39–41). Our speaker appears calm and rational, and the reader is often 'taken in' by Browning's speakers, in the sense that the story being told appears credible and valid. However, this is only up to a point; a Browning monologue always leaves the reader with a sense that there is a wider, ironic perspective to be had whereby the speaker must be considered again – sometimes shockingly anew – in the light of what his [sic] continuing narrative reveals about him. Hawlin also points out that 'what makes th[is] monologue chilling is the relationship between its achieved, verbal perfection and its disturbing subject matter' (Hawlin, 2002, p. 74). Although written as one block of text, the poem is written in tight iambic tetrameter (x / x / x / x /) and an ababb rhyme pattern. This verbal perfection is evidenced in the absolute balance of rhythm in the two halves of the line 'And strangled her. No pain felt she' (41).

Our speaker's murderous act is all the more unexpected because of his lack of agency in the first half of the poem. In many ways the 'action' in the poem is limited: movements made are small, circling round this macabre embrace. In a reversal of earlier, the speaker says 'I propped her head up as before, / Only, this time my shoulder bore / Her head, which droops upon it still' (49–51). We realize that the present moment of the poem's telling has been taking place with the strangled Porphyria draped over the speaker just as he describes. The repeated use of 'And' returns in the poem's final lines, linking them back to the highly sexualized lines earlier: 'And thus we sit together now, / And all night long we have not stirred, / And yet God has not said a word!' (58–60). The consummation of 'Porphyria's love' (56) is chillingly bloodless. Porphyria's lover ends by expressing surprise that God has not spoken. God has not spoken to condemn the act, nor to offer 'a divine note of congratulation' (Byron, 2003, p. 40). The poem is left enigmatic and unsettling.

'My Last Duchess'

The classic statement of the Victorian dramatic monologue regards it as involving a speaker/character, a scenario/setting, and an implied auditor. There is also an implied audience/reader, who hears or intuits more than the speaker intends. This definition has come from a reading of what is often regarded as the most representative of monologues, 'My Last Duchess' (1842). Byron cites Ina Beth Sessions' 1947 article, which suggested that Browning's most famous poem is the 'perfect' dramatic monologue (Byron, 2003, p. 8).

In 'Porphyria's Lover' the speaker does not ultimately seem to be talking to anyone. That may make sense, if we think he is mad. In 'My Last Duchess' the speaker of the poem is the Duke of Ferrara (a city in north Italy), and the time setting is the late Renaissance. The Duke is speaking to an envoy sent from another court to broker dowry arrangements for the Duke's next marriage. The poem is exemplary of Browning's skill in evoking character through colloquial, idiomatic speech. Part of the pleasure of 'My Last Duchess' is the interplay between the grammatical sense of sentences and the very frequent use of run-on lines, and the poetic structure of iambic pentameter couplets. Thirty-six of the fifty-six lines carry the sense over the line ending, but the rhyming end-words chime their rough music into the conversational tone.

The setting is evoked from the very start. We find ourselves in the cultured ambience of the Duke's court, as he shows off 'my last Duchess painted on the wall, / Looking as if she were alive' (1–2). The brilliance of this opening sentence, containing as it does the poem's title, is that it embodies the essence of the entire poem. It is only to be expected that a renaissance Duke would have had his wife's portrait painted and on the surface the Duke seems keen to point out how skilful the painting is, calling it a 'wonder' (3). But there is secretiveness and control evident in this display: '(since none puts by / The curtain I have drawn for you but I)' (9–10). We know what the envoy does, not because we have his words, or his actions described, but because the Duke's *response* implies it: 'not the first / Are you to turn and ask' (12–13) after 'The depth and passion of its earnest glance' (8). How did the painter Frà Pandolf 'call[ ] that spot / Of joy into the Duchess' cheek' (14–15)? How did he make her seem almost more alive than she was when she was alive? The Duke has a theory about this which starts to reveal more of his character, and we detect hints of jealously as the Duke imagines the compliments Frà Pandolf may have paid his wife as he looked on her beauty.

From line 21 the poem's attention shifts from the painting to the Duchess herself. Although the Duke is keen to control the extent to which men look at his former wife, the actual act of looking is not questioned. But when the roles are reversed it is a different matter: 'she liked whate'er / She looked on, and her looks went everywhere' (23–4). The problem with the Duchess, it seems, is that she lacked the rarified discrimination of her husband and did not fully appreci-ate that marrying him was effectively the same as being bought as another luxury item:

>   . . . all and each
> Would draw from her alike the approving speech,
> Or blush at least. She thanked men, – good! but thanked

> Somehow – I know not how – as if she ranked
> My gift of a nine-hundred-years-old name
> With anybody's gift.   (29–34)

Even more than in 'Porphyria's Lover' the reader is taken in. Our speaker is charming, disarming and eloquent. He is in fact a highly expert manipulator of rhetoric. When the Duke asks 'Who'd stoop to blame / This sort of trifling?' (34–5) as though his wife's generous 'approving speech' is nothing, the actual correct response is 'You would'. The more our speaker speaks, the more our sense of him shifts from sympathy to judgement, via the route of unease. When the Duke says that saying to his wife '"Just this / Or that in you disgusts me"' (37–8) would be 'stooping' (42) we realize that a very different psychological story is actually being told. The Duke is a man who 'choose[s] / Never to stoop' (42–3) and thus he 'gave commands' (45), and 'all smiles stopped together' (46).

The next lines – 'There she stands / As if alive. Will't please you rise?' (46–7) – take us back to the beginning and the very precise setting: the envoy sits and looks on the painting of the Duchess. The final section of the poem breaks away from the intensity of the narrative about the Duchess back to lighter pleasantries, but by this stage we are a good deal less comfortable. What, in fact, has the envoy been told? Has he not just witnessed a tour de force of masculine power to convey back to his master? The last nine lines of the poem contain vital information for the reader still piecing together all aspects of this monologue's scenario. In another brilliant touch the Duke says to the envoy 'Nay, we'll go / Together down, sir' (53–4), with the emphasis on *together*, as though the full implications of what the envoy has just heard are dawning on him and he either lingers, staring in horror at the painting a little too long, or has suddenly lost all desire to remain in the Duke's company. By the end of the poem the Duke has fully regained his composure and is once again showing off his art collection, but we now see that everything he says is laden with menace: 'Notice Neptune . . . Taming a sea-horse' (54–5). As Hawlin says, 'The feminine and the erotic have been reined in . . . The Duke has tamed his wife from an uncontrollable three dimensions to a very controllable two' (Hawlin, 2002, p. 69).

Browning's Italy: Art and historicism

Italy pervades many of Browning's dramatic monologues and some of his most famous love poems. Browning first visited Venice in 1838, and then returned to Italy in 1844. Most significantly it is where he eloped with Elizabeth Barrett after their secret marriage in 1846. They settled in Florence and lived in an apartment within Palazzo Guidi. This was the Brownings' main home until Barrett Browning's death in 1861, and only after this did Browning return to England. Browning said that Italy was his university, and the colour and warmth of the Italian landscape, as well as a sense of Italy as a place steeped in history – particularly the history of the Renaissance – pervade his poetry. Hawlin comments about *Men and Women* that the volume demonstrates 'the slow-working but profound impact of living in Florence after 1846' (Hawlin, 2002, p. 81). The first poem in the collection, 'Love Among the Ruins' encapsulates some of Browning's key themes, as well as showing off his metrical dexterity and skill with its stanzas of alternating long- and short-lined couplets. The speaker speaks from 'the site once of a city great and gay' (7), but now 'Such a carpet . . . this summer time, o'erspreads / And embeds / Every vestige . . .' (27–9). The entire ancient city is under grass: 'the single turret that remains . . . Marks the basement whence a tower in ancient time / Sprang sublime' (37, 43–4). This awareness of historical change and transience, of entire civilizations passing away, puts this poem in the same company as Shelley's 'Ozymandias' (1818) and D. G. Rossetti's 'The Burden of Nineveh' (1870). Where once the king 'looked upon the city, every side, / Far and wide' (61–2) from this turret, now the speaker's lover awaits him. Once this city represented a great world power, but all that is left after 'whole centuries of folly, noise and sin!' (81) is nature's gentle abundance. The 'patching houseleek's head of blossom winks / Through the chinks' (41–2) contains the same sexual suggestiveness as 'toadstools peep[ing] indulged' (65) in 'By the Fire-Side', and the poem's final three words – 'Love is best!' (84) – seem to turn away from all society in favour of the intimate consolations of the personal.

In Florence, Browning was living among the continuing legacy of the Renaissance via its artistic heritage. But the period could also be explored as a 'transitional moment' (Bristow, 1991, p. 87) in relation to the development of its art. The Pre-Raphaelite painters also embody in their name the same interest in transitional shifts between earlier and later Renaissance techniques. Both 'Fra Lippo Lippi' (1855) and 'Andrea del Sarto' (1855) focus on this shift.

'Fra Lippo Lippi'

In Georgio Vasari's *Lives of the Artists* (1550) Browning read of the exploits of the lusty painter Filippo Lippi, who, despite being a monk, was known to escape from the house of his patron, Cosimo de Medici, where he had been forcibly locked in to make him work harder. Browning's poem opens with Lippi being discovered by the Florentine police during the spring Carnival, 'at an alley's end / Where sportive ladies leave their doors ajar' (5–6). Through his engagingly colloquial speech – full of exclamations and breaking into song – he manages to win over the *sbirri* so that they don't arrest him, offering an account of his life and art along the way which doubles as Browning's aesthetic credo.

Lippi has been 'three weeks shut within my mew, / A-painting for the great man [i.e. Cosimo], saints and saints / And saints again' (47–9). The attractions of 'A sweep of lute-strings, laughs, and whiffs of song' (52) are what tempted him out. Lippi has an infectious and energetic love of the pleasures of this world – 'zooks, sir, flesh and blood, / That's all I'm made of!' (60–1) – and therein lies the paradox of being a sacred artist. Lippi was orphaned as a boy and taken into the monastery aged eight, but he considers the teaching he was given in vain as *'All the Latin I construe is, 'amo' I love!'* (111). Lippi's love of bodily things is the education that means he 'Found eyes and nose and chin for A's and B's' (132) and he is set to work painting frescos in the monastery. But Lippi's art is *too* real, *too* lifelike, and this brings him into conflict with the Prior, who says his job as an artist is to 'Paint the soul, never mind the legs and arms!' (193). What Browning is marking here is the shift from quattrocento art to the full-blown Renaissance techniques of Michelangelo, da Vinci and Raphael, or the shift from an artistic practice grounded in religious devotion (such as that of Giotto or Fra Angelico) to one that celebrates the human. Lippi uses real people as his models, including the Prior's very pretty niece:

> Suppose I've made her eyes all right and blue,
> Can't I take breath and try to add life's flash,
> And then add soul and heighten them threefold?   (212–14)

Browning puts some memorable lines into Lippi's lively mouth, which go right to the heart of his own intentions as a poet:

> . . . you've seen the world
> – The beauty and the wonder and the power,
> The shapes of things, their colours, lights and shades,
> Changes, surprises, – and God made it all!   (282–5)

For Browning the material must always win out over the ideal – indeed, the ideal is only apprehended through the physical. In Christian terms this means that Browning does not head into the anxious agnosticism of such as Tennyson, Clough and Arnold. In longer works such as *Christmas-Eve and Easter-Day* (1850) and 'Bishop Blougram's Apology' (1855) his response to contemporary religious debates is 'to suspect that the new thinking did not simply invalidate older currents of religious thought and feeling' (Hawlin, 2002, p. 89). It is art that can make human beings realize how amazing the world is: 'we're made so that we love / First when we see them painted, things we have passed / Perhaps a hundred times nor cared to see' (300–2). Lippi's delight in the physical is actually a spiritual commitment: 'This world's no blot for us, / Nor blank; it means intensely, and means good' (313–14). Ultimately Lippi says he will 'make amends' (343) for his misdemeanours by painting 'Something in Sant' Ambrogio's!' (346), only his roguish sense of fun means he intends to paint *himself* into the devotional picture: 'Mazed, motionless and moonstruck – I'm the man!' (364). In a brilliant dénouement which mimics the poem's debates about the lifelikeness of art Lippi imagines this self-portrait coming to life and being slightly overwhelmed at the 'pure company' (368) in which he finds himself. He looks for a way out – 'a corner for escape' (369) – but is stopped by 'a sweet angelic slip of a thing'

(370) who says he has a rightful place in the holy painting because saints are generally no good with a paintbrush. In the real Lippi's *Coronation of the Virgin* (1441–7, Uffizi Gallery) the painter kneels in the bottom right of the picture.

'Andrea del Sarto'

Vasari's *Lives of the Artists* is also the source of the back story to 'Andrea del Sarto'. Vasari considered del Sarto a painter with faultless technique, but hampered by a weakness of spirit and a demanding wife. This poem is an exploration of artistic and moral failure as del Sarto never becomes as great a painter as he could be. The implied auditor is Lucrezia, del Sarto's wife. She often sat as her husband's model and throughout the poem del Sarto is busy sketching her. The poem opens with del Sarto wishing not to 'quarrel any more' (1) with his wife and agreeing to 'work for your friend's friend' (5) on a painting. The meaning behind the meaning however, is that del Sarto is being distracted from his highest calling as an artist to achieve greater things. He appears almost complacent about his abilities and knows that he can do, technically, what other artists find difficult: 'I do what many dream of, all their lives, / – Dream? Strive to do, and agonize to do, / And fail in doing' (69–71). But del Sarto is only too aware that there is a cost to his complacency: 'There burns a truer light of God in them, / . . . than goes to prompt / This low-pulsed forthright craftsman's hand of mine' (79, 81–2). In his own work 'A common greyness silvers everything' (35). Del Sarto is a very different kind of speaker from Porphyria's lover or the Duke of Ferrara, but he is still divided from himself, in being 'convinced of and yet resistant to his own failure' (Pearsall, 2000, p. 82). As with the unknown and unremembered painter of an earlier poem, 'Pictor Ignotus' (1845), his measure of comparison is with the Renaissance 'greats' Raphael, Michelangelo and da Vinci.

Lucrezia as the addressee of del Sarto's monologue is crucial to our understanding of it, as his vexed relationship with her is one of the justifications he offers for his failure to be the painter he might have been: 'Had you . . . given me soul', he says to her, 'We might have risen to Rafael, I and you!' (118–19). Between these lines and the next it seems Lucrezia answers back as del Sarto continues 'Nay, Love, you did give all I asked, I think – / More than I merit, yes, by many times' (120–1). Note the hesitancy of 'I think'. The poem also functions as a reflection on (early) Victorian constructions of artistic manliness. Unlike Fra Lippo Lippi, del Sarto *isn't* a monk. Herbert Sussman has discussed how 'the monk becomes the extreme or limit case of the central problematic in the Victorian practice of masculinity, the proper regulation of an innate male energy' (Sussman, 1995, p. 3). Del Sarto is conscious that the painters with which he compares himself are not married. He imagines being given 'one more chance' (260) in heaven:

> Four great walls in the New Jerusalem,
> Meted on each side by the angel's reed,
> For Leonard, Rafael, Agnolo and me
> To cover – the three first without a wife,
> While I have mine!   (261–5)

Sussman comments on Browning's model of masculinity in which 'art-making, love-making and money-making are valued as signs of true manliness, productive expressions of natural, God-given male energy' (Sussman, 1995, p. 84). Del Sarto is not doing any of these very successfully. So, ultimately, in the poem's most famous lines, del Sarto is all too aware that 'a man's reach should exceed his grasp, / Or what's a heaven for?' (97–8).

Browning's dangerous edge

Browning does not completely eschew contemporary settings: 'Bishop Blougram's Apology' imagines a worldly Roman Catholic bishop in dialogue with a journalist, Mr. Gigadibs, who does not understand how the Bishop can maintain his belief in Christianity in the modern world. Although this monologue might appear to be exposing the hypocrisy of how well the bishop has done out of his apostolic calling, 'the more we engage with [it] . . . the harder it seems to make easy judgements of approval and condemnation' (Hawlin, 2002, p. 91). The bishop eloquently takes on the journalist's commitment to unbelief over his commitment to belief. Similarly 'Mr Sludge "The Medium"' (1864) mocks a rogue spiritualist (the Brownings had attended a séance in 1855) but is also an extended discussion of truth and falsehood. Although Sludge admits that he deals in 'Strictly . . . what good people style untruth' (188) he makes an idiosyncratic and amusing attempt to justify how 'tables do tip / In the oddest way of themselves: and pens, good Lord, / Who knows if you drive them or they drive you?' (195–7). Sludge recognizes the attractions of lying – 'hang th[e] truth, / It spoils all dainties proffered in its place!' (385–6) – and his challenge to the 'distinguished man' (462) who has hired him is whether he has never indulged in any 'imposture[s]' (545) of his own. Sludge's slippery charm means that he is able to make 'The limpid nature, the unblemished life, / The spotless honour' (727–28) look rather dull, and he appears surprised that 'I somehow vomit truth to-day' (808).

There is tremendous wit, vivacity, and energy in Browning's poetry. In later life, once he had ceased to be 'Mrs Barrett Browning', Browning would dine with Prime Minister Gladstone and even had his own literary society: the Browning Society was established in 1881 and still exists to this day (see caricaturist Max Beerbohm's *Robert Browning, Taking Tea with the Browning Society* for a wry take on the adoration Browning garnered in his later years [Beerbohm, 1904]). In many ways Browning was the antithesis of the broody, moody Romantic or Tennysonian poet, and his sociable affability might even suggest a certain blandness. But it is Bishop Blougram who must have the last word in articulating another of Browning's poetic creeds:

> Our interest's on the dangerous edge of things.
> The honest thief, the tender murderer,
> The superstitious atheist, demirep
> That loves and saves her soul in new French books –
> We watch while these in equilibrium keep
> The giddy line midway . . .   (395–400)

Browning's achieved intention in his monologues is to 'keep the line' (401) – the 'dangerous edge' – that divides his characters from themselves.

Reading

Bristow, Joseph (1991), *Robert Browning*. New York: St. Martin's Press.

Hawlin, Stefan (2002), *Robert Browning*. London: Routledge.

Pearsall, Cornelia D. J. (2000), 'The dramatic monologue', in *The Cambridge Companion to Victorian Poetry*, ed. Joseph Bristow, pp. 67–88. Cambridge: Cambridge University Press.

Sussman, Herbert (1995), *Victorian Masculinities: Manhood and Masculine Poetics in Early Victorian Literature and Art*. Cambridge: Cambridge University Press.

Research

- The Browning monologue famously opens up an ironic gap between speaker and reader. Offer a reading of one of Browning's monologues paying attention to how irony functions in it.

- How would you read any of Browning's monologues in the context of (early) Victorian masculinities?

- Why are Browning's speakers all mad or bad (or both)? What does this add?

5

Elizabeth Barrett Browning
and *Aurora Leigh*

The first woman poet

'**E**lizabeth Barrett Browning is for most practical purposes the first woman poet in English literature' (Mermin, 1989, p. 1), and her relationship to immediate female predecessors was ambiguous. Although she paid tribute to Felicia Hemans and Letitia Landon she also 'attempt[ed] to clear a space for herself as a new type of woman poet and to be defining herself against the traditions of women's poetry' thus established. As Simon Avery continues, despite their popularity Landon and Hemans contributed to 'a legacy of disabling and inhibiting assumptions about the role of the woman poet which was subsequently hard to dislodge' (Avery and Stott, 2003, pp. 3, 4). In a famous letter of 1845 Barrett Browning wrote 'England has had many learned women . . . and yet where were the poetesses? . . . I look everywhere for Grandmothers & see none' (Avery and Stott, 2003, p. 3).

Barrett Browning became one of the period's most acclaimed poets: a potential candidate for the Poet Laureateship in 1850, she outweighed her husband in popularity and success during her lifetime. Christina Rossetti said she was the 'Great Poetess of our own day' in the preface to 'Monna Innominata' (1881), itself inspired by Barrett Browning's 'Sonnets from the Portuguese' (1850). Dora Greenwell wrote two celebratory sonnets, 'To Elizabeth Barrett Browning, in

1851' and 'To Elizabeth Barrett Browning, in 1861'; Bessie Rayner Parkes expressed admiration in 'To Elizabeth Barrett Browning' (1852); and Dinah Craik wrote 'To Elizabeth Barrett Browning on Her Later Sonnets. 1856' (1881).

The development of Elizabeth Barrett Browning

Women conventionally lacked the classical education which meant they could enter into the poetic traditions to which men had access. Elizabeth Barrett, however, gained an unusually liberal and wide-ranging home education, let loose among her father's library. She was fluent in numerous languages, including Greek. By thirteen she had written her first epic poem, 'The Battle of Marathon'. Marjorie Stone emphasizes Barrett Browning's 'audacity of authorship' (Stone, 1995, p. 55) in that she clearly wished to become a poet (*not* poetess). She was shaped by Romantic conceptions which assumed 'the poet' was male, but absolutely refused to accept these constraints. She believed strongly in the Romantic tradition of the poet as prophet: in *Aurora Leigh* Aurora says poets are 'the only truth-tellers now left to God, / The only speakers of essential truth' (1:859–60).

Her first collection was *An Essay on Mind* (1826), and her growing reputation was consolidated by *Poems* (1844). The latter volume was published in America as *A Drama of Exile, and Other Poems*, and 'A Drama in Exile' reworks that most famous of English epics, John Milton's *Paradise Lost* (1667), revisiting Adam and Eve's banishment from the Garden of Eden with a special focus on Eve. The volume also contains 'A Vision of Poets', in which the poet's calling contains a necessary suffering. The gravity with which Barrett Browning took her own vocation as poet is seen in the preface to *Poems*: 'Poetry has been as serious a thing to me as life itself; and life has been a very serious thing . . . I never mistook pleasure for the final cause of poetry; nor leisure, for the hour of the poet' (Barrett Browning, 1893, p. xi).

Life, indeed, had been a serious thing and an experience of suffering to the young Elizabeth Barrett, who contracted a tubercular illness in the late 1830s. Her beloved brother Edward ('Bro') also drowned in 1840. If you harbour an image of a Victorian woman fainting languidly on a sofa it may have originated – however obliquely – from the mythologizing of Elizabeth Barrett as an invalid. This started at the same time that Barrett Browning's poetic reputation was establishing itself. In 1844 the poet and commentator Richard Horne published *A New Spirit of the Age*, following on from Hazlitt's *The Spirit of the Age* (1825). Horne updated Hazlitt's character sketches of contemporary figures of note, including one on 'Miss E. B. Barrett'. As Horne was a good friend of Barrett Browning and it is known that she contributed to the work, it is hard not to think she knew of the description of her as 'Confined entirely to her own apartment, and almost hermetically sealed, in consequence of some extremely delicate state of health' (Horne, 1907, p. 339). However, five years on the sofa gave Barrett Browning lots of time to read.

Poems also contains 'To Flush, My Dog' and the sonnet 'Flush or Faunus'. Both were no doubt grist to the mill of R. M. Leonard's later anthology *The Dog in British Poetry* (1893). The sonnet is cautionary tale enough why it is not wise to compare your pets to figures from classical legend. Flush, Barrett Browning's beloved cocker spaniel, was dog-napped in 1843 and 1846 by organized thieves from the East End of London. Barrett Browning's tenacity and willingness to defy her somewhat tyrannical father were demonstrated in her going behind his back to organize the ransom that got Flush back the first time, and the second time she ventured into the depths of Shoreditch from rarified Wimpole Street to secure his release.

Elizabeth, Robert and Italy

Elizabeth Barrett met Robert Browning (and vice versa) through their poetry before they ever met each other. Browning's first letter, in January 1845, contains the effusive lines, 'I love your verses with all my heart, dear Miss Barrett . . . and I love you too' (Mermin, 1989, p. 116). This looks like the same 'woman equals poem' conflation that so damned Victorian women's poetry, but in his second letter it is clear Browning envies the self-expressiveness allowed to women poets: 'You speak out, *you* – I only make men and women speak'

(Mermin, 1989, p. 122). Barrett Browning was an early admirer of Browning's poetry when critics were not, so a mutual appreciation of each other's talent is at the heart of one of the most well-known literary love affairs. Robert and Elizabeth engaged in a voluminous, spirited correspondence from 1845–6 (see Karlin, 1985, 1989). Edward Barrett Moulton-Barrett, Elizabeth's patriarch of a father, not only forbade her, but *all* of his children from marrying. So they married in secret, on 12 September 1846, and eloped to Italy, living in Florence until Barrett Browning's death in 1861.

The warm Italian air suited Barrett Browning better than the fogs of London, but the heat of Italy pervades her work too, and is an important backdrop to *Aurora Leigh*. Barrett Browning's politically libertarian instincts are also seen in *Casa Guidi Windows* (1851) which charted the Italian 'Risorgimento' (resurgence) movement seeking Italian unification free from Austrian governance. 'Casa Guidi' was the name given by Barrett Browning to the apartment in Palazzo Guidi, where the Brownings lived. *Poems Before Congress* (1860) was published the same year Italy achieved reunification.

Aurora Leigh: Introduction

Aurora Leigh (pub. November 1856; dated 1857) is often described as a verse novel and translates some of the concerns of the contemporary novel into extended poetic form. Works such as Clough's *Amours de Voyage* (1855), Meredith's *Modern Love* (1862) and Browning's *The Ring and the Book* (1868) could also be classed similarly (Felluga, 2002), but *Aurora Leigh* was one of the most popular. The first edition sold out in a week, the second in a month, and by 1900 twenty editions had been reprinted. Like the Victorian novel the work is attentive to character development over time, incorporates dialogue, creates a realistic setting, and engages with pressing social and political issues of the day. But also, importantly, 'its heightened, highly charged feeling and language . . . are overtly "poetical"; and the fact that it is a poem is an essential part of its meaning. It is about writing poetry, and it *is* the kind of poem it describes' (Mermin, 1989, p. 185).

Barrett Browning's understanding of poetry as the most prized literary form meant she 'aspired to the composition of the highest kind of poem, an epic. She wanted poetry to deal with life as fully as prose fiction did, but without sacrificing its generic superiority' (Mermin, 1989, p. 186). Epic was traditionally a very masculine genre, celebrating male heroism (see Tennyson's *Idylls of the King* [1858–85] and William Morris's *The Story of Sigurd the Volsung and the Fall of the Niblungs* [1876]), but *Aurora Leigh* makes a star-lit female character its central consciousness. Western European narrative poetry traced its origins back to the epic poet Homer, and *Aurora Leigh* 'imagin[es] how a woman could become the feminine of Homer . . . with a woman poet as hero and her country's destiny hanging in the balance of her deeds. Its argument is that writing a poem can itself be an epic action that leads . . . to the creation of a new social order' (Mermin, 1989, p. 183).

Other long poems hover in the background: Tennyson's mock-heroic *The Princess* (1847) and Clough's *The Bothie of Tober-na-Vuolich* (1848) are also concerned with women's education and the 'Condition of England' question of the 1840s and 1850s. Wordsworth's *The Prelude* (1850) is another example of not only bildungsroman (focussing on the maturation of the hero/heroine) but also *kunstler*roman (concerned with the growth of the *artist*). Ultimately, however, *Aurora Leigh* is its own distinctive work.

Aurora Leigh: Books I to III

Aurora Leigh's opening line – 'Of writing many books there is no end' (I. 1) introduces a work which has at its centre a woman who becomes a writer. It is written in blank verse and breaks are introduced rather like paragraphs in prose – hence the organization of ideas influences form over any set stanzaic pattern. Can Victorian poetry encompass the novelistic range that Barrett Browning wants it to have? As Mermin says, 'Perhaps the greatest inadequacy of Victorian poetry was its narrow range of diction, which usually could not accommodate simple prosaic things' (Mermin, 1989, p. 216). A review of *Aurora Leigh* in *Blackwood's Edinburgh Magazine* (January 1857) printed out passages as blocks of prose to suggest they sounded slightly ridiculous. The reviewer's point is that 'All poetical characters, all poetical situations, must be idealized.

The language [of poetry] is not that of common life' (Reynolds, 1996, p. 416). Barrett Browning challenges this view.

Book I introduces Aurora's childhood. Her Italian, Florentine mother died when she was four, and Aurora's 'mother-want' (l. 40) pervades the poem. Her father, an 'austere Englishman' (l. 65), fell passionately in love with her mother, and Aurora is a product of this symbolic union, the warmth of the South melting the coolness of the North. She is brought up among the maternal hills of Pelago. At thirteen, as Aurora 'awoke / To full life and life's needs and agonies' (l. 207–8), her father dies, leaving her with the command, 'Love, my child, love, love!' (l. 212).

Aurora then moves to England, to be brought up by her aunt. The 'frosty cliffs' (l. 251) anticipate the emotional landscape to come and Barrett Browning is damning about the limited education given to young women:

> I learnt a little algebra, a little
> Of the mathematics, – brushed with extreme flounce
> The circle of the sciences . . .
> . . . .
>   I washed in
> Landscapes from nature (rather say, washed out).
> I danced the polka and Cellarius [a waltz],
> Spun glass, stuffed birds, and modelled flowers in wax,
> Because she liked accomplishments in girls.   (l. 403–5, 422–6)

Aurora is astute about how such 'accomplishments' are actually valued, linking the superfluous items that middle-class women sew to a critique of seamstresses' pay, because the 'worth of our work' (l. 465) is so little.

We first hear of Romney Leigh, Aurora's cousin, as 'early master of Leigh Hall' (l. 516). He is a passing note on the way to fine descriptions of the English landscape. This is *not* a Romantic, sublime setting, but 'A nature tamed / And grown domestic' (l. 634–5), which nonetheless rejuvenates Aurora. She is also sustained by 'Books, books, books!' (l. 832), and initiated into the masculine world of ideas through finding 'the secret of a garret-room / Piled high with cases in my father's name' (l. 833–4). Book I's most rapturous writing is reserved for Aurora's discovery of poetry. When she says 'my soul, / At poetry's divine first finger-touch, / Let go conventions and sprang up surprized' (I. 850–2) the sexual energy appropriated is masculine. If the space marked out for the 'poet' in the earlier Victorian period is gendered male then any woman who enters that space must inevitably draw upon the masculine language which delineates it. But in doing this, Barrett Browning transforms the meaning of poet to become a precursive foremother for other women poets who follow her. Although Aurora's early poems are derivative, the 'inner life' (I. 1027) of poetry developing in her is a spiritual formation of the 'soul' (I. 1031).

Thus far *Aurora Leigh* is tangentially linked to aspects of Barrett Browning's life: 'the author's life is essential not only to the poem's genesis but also to its public meaning. Since hers was the only example of such a life that her readers would have known . . . the personal application could hardly have been avoided' (Mermin, 1989, p. 220). However, autobiographical readings should not be applied too literally to a plot as fictional as that of any Victorian social-problem novel. Aurora and Romney are less Elizabeth and Robert than Elizabeth and Darcy from *Pride and Prejudice*, not least in the spirited dialogues between them in Book II and in that both have to overcome a degree of pride in their own worldview and prejudice about that of the other.

Aurora marks her coming of age by crowning herself with ivy. Romney sees this and a sustained debate follows about men, women, work and art. Romney's view of women's inferiority means they cannot be poets:

> Women as you are,
> Mere women, personal and passionate,
> You give us doating mothers, and perfect wives,
> Sublime Madonnas, and enduring saints!
> We get no Christ from you, – and verily
> We shall not get a poet, in my mind.   (II. 220–5)

Other of Romney's instincts are more laudable: he has a keen sense of what Disraeli referred to in his novel *Sibyl* (1845) as the 'Two nations . . . THE RICH AND THE POOR' (Disraeli, 1981, pp. 65–6) and the gulf between them. The 'great cure' (II. 281) lies in social action. Before we know it, Romney has proposed to Aurora and been rejected. 'You have a wife already . . .' says Aurora, 'Your social theory' (II. 409–10). One target in *Aurora Leigh* is Charles Fourier (1772–1837) who sought the reconstruction of society via communal associations or 'phalansteries'. Romney sets one up on Leigh Hall estate. Barrett Browning's objection to such an idea – and this French form of socialism more generally – is that it entails the loss of individualism.

Aurora makes her own passionate plea for the 'vocation' (II. 455) of the artist. Romney embodies a mid-Victorian, middle-class, male view of gendered relations, as he 'sees a woman as the complement / Of his sex merely' (II. 435–6). Aurora rejects this but is aware of the heroism in his social altruism, and here we see the influence of Thomas Carlyle. A portrait of Carlyle (effectively by Barrett Browning) appears in *A New Spirit of the Age* and he is portrayed as a poet-prophet, speaking necessary truths to his times. But it is a core aim of the work to make very clear that Romney's faulty view of both women and poetry cannot be redeemed by any of his other good intentions. Aurora's aunt accuses Aurora of 'groping in the dark' (II. 585) in refusing Romney, and metaphors of light and sight, seeing and *in*sight (and their converse of not seeing and blindness) abound in the poem.

Undeterred by a mere woman's no, Romney proposes again, but a note to Aurora that says 'Henceforth, my flower . . . Write women's verses and dream women's dreams' (II. 828, 832) was never going to succeed. Aurora's aunt dies, leaving her no money, but Romney attempts to give Aurora the money left to the Leigh Estate himself. Aurora refuses it. She moves to London and transforms into a self-made professional writer, living in a garret in Kensington, west London. 'Get leave to work / In this world – 'tis the best you get at all' (III. 161–2), says Aurora. This chimes strongly with a mid-Victorian work ethic, but has far more resonance because women were barred from most meaningful paid work. Feminist campaigner Barbara Bodichon, co-founder of Girton College, Cambridge, cited *Aurora Leigh* in her 1857 pamphlet *Women and Work*.

Book III introduces other key characters. Romney is the love interest for three women, who represent different class positions. His upper-class suitor is the sophisticated and artificial Lady Waldemar. She feigns interest in Romney's causes, but draws the line at 'wearing gowns / Provided by the Ten Hours' movement' (III. 601), a nineteenth-century equivalent of fair-trade clothing. Romney, however, is now set on marrying a seamstress, Marian Erle, in order to unite the disparate classes. Aurora refuses to enter into Lady Waldemar's scheme to break up the marriage, saying 'I love love' (III. 702).

Nevertheless Aurora does venture out to visit Marian, occasioning a notorious portrayal of a working-class environment. The people are viewed as grotesque:

> A woman, rouged
> Upon the angular cheek-bones, kerchief torn,
> Thin dangling locks, and flat lascivious mouth,
> Cursed at a window . . .   (III. 764–7)

Marian – 'This daughter of the people' (III. 806) – escapes such mob caricature. As Mermin says, 'Aurora [or, Barrett Browning] is appalled by the poor in general – baffled by their brute misery, terrified by their hostility and violence. They haunt the poem with the demonic vitality of nightmare' (Mermin, 1989, p. 203). Marian, however, is a paragon of working-class purity, miraculously unsullied. Born in the shadow of the Malvern Hills, Worcestershire (more maternal hills), Marian's father drinks and her mother takes it out on her, eventually trying to sell her to a squire. This causes her to run away, and in a fever she ends up in hospital, where she is visited by one Romney Leigh . . . who takes pity on her and sends her to a 'famous sempstress-house' (III. 1231) in London. Marian is also portrayed as one of the 'good' working class through the ennobling effects of education, having heard 'a lecture at an institute' (III. 997). Reading has 'carried in / To her soul' (III. 1006–7).

Aurora Leigh: Books IV and V

Book IV opens with Marian dropping tears onto her current piece of sewing, which happens to be Lady Waldemar's new dress

(IV. 27). Romney's marriage proposal, with its high aim of effecting a nuptial union of the divided classes, is not something the writing endorses. Marian 'Look[s] blindly in his face' (IV. 118), and her inherent class subservience is stressed through imagery of her as an innocent-but-startled woodland animal. She is described as akin to a bird, a deer, a squirrel. Worst of all, she is 'doglike' (IV. 281) when Romney appears as Aurora is visiting Marian, threatening to turn into his very own Flush. Romney offers to escort Aurora back out of the 'hideous streets' (IV. 387) and their lively, well-matched banter is emphasized.

We sit in the pew with Aurora as guests arrive for the wedding. On the one side the inhabitants of St. Margaret's Court 'ooze[ ] into the church / In a dark slow stream, like blood' (IV. 553–4). On the other we overhear all the latest upper-class gossip. The opinions that Romney has 'turned quite lunatic upon / This modern question of the poor' and that 'if we stand not by our [class] order, we / In England, we fall headlong' (IV. 662–3, 670–1) may well be close to Barrett Browning's own. The bride is fashionably late . . . allowing Aurora to paint a portrait of the other upper-class character in the work, Lord Howe. He too is influenced by French radical ideas, but thinks this marriage is being used 'to instruct us formally / To fill the ditches up 'twixt class and class' (IV. 754–5).

Once apparent that the bride has had second thoughts, working-class distrust of the upper classes erupts into a wholescale riot. Barrett Browning portrays the mob as a pack of hounds tearing Romney's futile placatory words to pieces. *Aurora Leigh* is not short on moments of melodrama, and if a bride who fails to show and a riot aren't enough, these are topped by Aurora launching herself into the fray 'Head-foremost to the rescue of my soul' (IV. 875) just as Romney is about to be eaten alive. This moment – when Aurora lets slip that she and Romney are two souls who are one in her own mind – shows the influence of eighteenth-century philosopher-mystic Emanuel Swedenborg (1688–1772). Reform for Swedenborg is about overcoming the dualism of spirit/body, heaven/ earth in the greater cause of love. The drama of the moment also evokes Margaret Hale shielding John Thornton from the angry strikers outside his factory in Gaskell's *North and South* (1855). Marian writes to Romney, without really explaining her change of mind, but she recognizes that Aurora is 'ah, most like you!' (IV. 939). In dialogue with Romney Aurora offers impassioned lines on the power of art, which 'pushes toward the intense significance / Of all things, hungry for the Infinite' (IV. 1155–6).

Book V opens with nine rhetorical questions. Aurora asks with what will her poems 'speak . . . in mysterious tune' (V. 2), taking in the entire cosmos, nature's seasons, and human cycles of life and death. The imagining of such possibilities makes Aurora's opening riposte to 'be humble' (V. 1) almost comic. By contrast, the man she wants to impress with her poetry finds her 'Too light a book for a grave man's reading!' (V. 41). Book V is at the centre of *Aurora Leigh's* structure and is its 'spiritual' heart, setting out Barrett Browning's poetic philosophy. Aurora speaks of the poet's need to give 'human meanings' (V. 126) to 'the earth / The body of our body' (V. 116–17) – to make it come alive with a human vitality, rather than creating 'book[s] / Of surface-pictures' (V. 130–1). This is very much a pre-Darwinian relation to the natural world.

The most famous passages concern the strong assertion of poetry's continuing necessity and relevance (see Chapter 2). Epic is still a living genre, but Aurora deflates its grandeur by saying Homer's characters were actually just like the men and women of her own day: 'Helen [of Troy's] hair turned grey / Like any plain Miss Smith' (V. 147–8). The converse is that 'all men [are] possible heroes' (V. 152). Aurora is well aware of the view that the present is an unheroic 'pewter age' (V. 160) and 'An age of scum, spooned off the richer past' (V. 161), but she 'distrust[s] the poet who discerns / No character or glory in his times' (V. 189–90). The poet's 'sole work is to represent the age, / Their age, not Charlemagne's, – this live, throbbing age' (V. 202–3). The language in this passage almost pulsates with the passionate heartbeat of its speaker. Epic is energized and transformed here via contemporary Victorian words which speak its modernity: why should 'gaberdines' (V. 162) and 'modern varnish' (V. 208) and 'Fleet Street' (V. 213) not be part of epic now, asks Aurora. The poet's task is to 'Never flinch, / But still, unscrupulously epic, catch / Upon the burning lava of a song / The full-veined, heaving, double-breasted Age' (V. 213–16). The here-and-now is imagined as the breathing, panting body of a woman. It is an unashamedly adult – even sexual – image. It is the poet's task to communicate this newly feminized age, which women are starting to change for good, and it cannot be understood aside from them.

Aurora is less conclusive about 'What form is best' (V. 223) in poetry. She suggests that the inner pulsions of content will influence form: 'Keep up the fire, / And leave the generous flames to shape themselves' (V. 235–6). Form is certainly not meant to 'imprison' (V. 226) in this poetic philosophy.

So Aurora's magnum opus is written (V. 352), but the cost of great art is suffering. The artist's gift is in 'turning outward, with a sudden wrench, / Half agony, half ecstasy, the thing / He feels the inmost' (V. 370–2). In spite of being 'flushed with praise' (V. 429), Aurora is also 'sad' (V. 399). The solitary female artist who writes of a passion she does not personally experience is evoked: 'To have our books / Appraised by love, associated with love, / While *we* sit loveless!' (V. 474–6). *Aurora Leigh* is not a poem to deny its female longings: 'We're hungry', says Aurora (V. 488). She wants to write *and* to love.

It is eighteen months since Aurora last saw Romney, and he has since converted Leigh Hall into almshouses. Line 549 brings us into the present moment (everything previous has been a retelling of the past) as we learn that Aurora 'went to-night' (V. 580) to a soirée at Lord Howe's. She observes the women present – his gracious but cold aristocratic wife, and the 'full-breathed beauty' (V. 624) of Lady Waldemar, whom Romney is now soon to marry – and overhears two students considering Lady Waldemar's suitability as 'Leigh's disciple' (V. 778). Aurora appears an outsider here: becoming a fêted poet has almost desexed her and she is aware of standing apart from the more usual mass of womanhood. Aurora's friendship with Lord Howe is one of the most equal and comfortable relationships in the work, perhaps because he is no sexual suitor. They speak to each other 'man to man' (V. 811). He also brings a marriage proposal from one John Eglinton in Kent, who is 'A reputable man, / An excellent landlord of the olden stamp' (V. 869–70). However, the letter is 'stereotyped' (V. 898), meaning it has been printed on plate metal and can be easily reproduced, and Aurora is merely one of many trophy actresses, dancers and singers Eglinton has approached. Lord Howe gently suggests that 'A happy life means prudent compromise' (V. 923) and that it may be necessary 'For art's sake, [to] pause'

(V. 951), if she wishes to find love. As with Romney's rejected proposal, this prompts a principled response from Aurora.

The evening ends with Lady Waldemar engaging Aurora in conversation, with every word calculated to say more than its surface intention. Lady Waldemar has taken on Romney's view that reading *precedes* action, and we witness the sadistic enjoyment she obtains from her condescension towards Aurora the poet. Back home a highly sexually charged scene follows with Aurora loosening her tight clothing and hair and wishing that 'I could but unloose my soul!' (V. 1039). This dramatizes the repression of feeling necessary, and the book ends with Aurora writing a congratulatory letter to Lady Waldemar, but also signalling her intention to leave England again for 'my Italy, / My own hills!' (V. 1266–7). Once again a rejected proposal precipitates Aurora to make a physical move, this time back to the comfort of the motherland.

Aurora Leigh: Books VI to IX

Aurora is now in Paris, and after an opening defence of 'this noble France, / This poet of the nations' (VI. 53–4), and a fine evocation of the city (78ff.) she spots what seems to be either Romney or Marian in the crowd: 'What a face, what a look, what a likeness!' (VI. 232). It is actually Marian, and Aurora sees that she has a child. This introduces the social problem that *Aurora Leigh* cares most about – the fallen woman. Aurora is quick to jump to conclusions, 'cruel like the rest' (VI. 367); nonetheless she is determined to 'save her' (VI. 388), employing the usual Christian language of redemption. When she does track Marian down she admits she has 'hungered after [her] more than bread' (VI. 454) and offers her 'a home for you / And me and no one else' (VI. 458–9). Mermin describes this scene as if Aurora is 'proposing marriage' (Mermin, 1989, p. 193) and while this work does have an ostensible heterosexual romance plot, an equivalent emotional response to any caused by Romney is produced in Aurora in response to other female characters.

Marian takes Aurora to her lodgings, which are 'Scarce larger than a grave' (VI. 552). Aurora initially wants to judge Marian, but faced with the child (and hence Marian's redeeming motherhood) 'Love was here / In an instant' (VI. 574–5), and we recall the pre-eminence of the command to love in Aurora's own philosophy. Marian passionately refutes the suggestion that she was complicit in having a child out of wedlock: 'I was not ever . . . seduced, / But simply, murdered' (VI. 770–1). This declaration of innocence is enough to cause Aurora to ask pardon from 'Sweet holy Marian!' (VI. 782), whose name evokes the Virgin Mary.

An account follows of Marian's awkwardness as Romney's fiancée, and how her discomfort increased 'from the day / The gracious lady [Waldemar] paid a visit first' (VI. 970–1). Lady Waldemar was clearly up to tricks in visiting Marian, telling her 'Romney could not love me' (VI. 1014), and she 'promised kindly to provide the means, / With instant passage to the colonies' (VI. 1128–9), removing Marian out of the way in favour of her own designs on Romney. Lady Waldemar is thus indirectly responsible for Marian's subsequent rape, in France where she ends up. An incisive comment is given to Marian when she says 'We wretches cannot tell out all our wrong / Without offence to decent happy folk' (VI. 1220–1), but Barrett Browning does offer a working-class woman's account of being raped that lays the blame firmly in 'man's violence' (VI. 1226). Some reviewers of *Aurora Leigh* took offence at this, as they had with Gaskell's *Ruth* (1853), but Barrett Browning's commitment to speaking out women's truths is not in doubt here.

Marian is taken in by 'A miller's wife at Clichy' (VII. 14) and found a servant's post. She is so innocent that she does not realize she could be pregnant and ultimately is dismissed. Once her child is born she becomes a sempstress (connecting back to Book III). Back in the present Aurora proposes (literally?) to Marian that they should live together in Italy with her son and 'two mothers shall / Make . . . up to him' for any absence of a father (VII. 124–5). Aurora contemplates writing to Romney about Lady Waldemar, decides not to, and then lets slip (although not in Marian's presence) 'I will not let thy hideous secret out / To agonize the man I love – I mean / The friend I love' (VII. 172–4). Aurora does however write to Lord Howe, asking him to tell Romney Marian is found, and writes to Lady Waldemar blaming her for Marian's downfall and threatening that if she wrongs Romney as his wife then she will 'open mouth, / And such a noise will follow' (VII. 366–7).

Aurora is forced to revise her attitudes towards fallen women in *Aurora Leigh*, and as in numerous literary works of the period which portray a middle-class response to a prostitute or unmarried mother, the character whose attitudes change is a surrogate for the implied reader. Looking on the sleeping Marian and her babe the night before they travel to the warm embrace of the Tuscan hills, 'There seemed no sin, no shame, no wrath, no grief' (VII. 385).

Once in Italy Aurora receives news from England via her artist friend Vincent Carrington. Her poetry has been well received back home. If the reader starts to think another artist might be an appropriate suitor for Aurora this prospect is quashed immediately as Vincent brings news of his own impending marriage – to one of his models. This represents another unequal partnership. Aurora does not want to be any man's muse. Vincent also tells Aurora that Romney has been struck down with fever. The heat of Italy is evoked again as Aurora stifles her emotions in the blunt assumption that 'he's married; that is clear' (VII. 675). An extended reflection on both truth and art's power to transform follow: 'If man could feel, / Not one day, in the artist's ecstasy, / But every day . . . / Henceforward he would paint the globe with wings' (VII. 857–9, 862). The visionary artist remains essential to Aurora's conception of human transformation.

But Italy this time is not what it was previously. The hot summer is now oppressive and Aurora misses her dead father, returning to her childhood home only to find it unrecognizable. She wanders the Tuscan streets, imagining the lives of the poor Italian women she sees outside churches, but she 'did not write, nor read, nor even think' (VII. 1306). The very last word of the book is 'lost' (VII. 1311).

The final two books are almost entirely concerned with steering the plot towards its heterosexual romance conclusion. So although Book VIII opens with an image of Aurora and Marian's peaceful, settled life, this is soon disrupted. In a psychoanalytically-influenced reading Mermin suggests that the maternal imagery of *Aurora Leigh* which 'defines the quest for the mother as a yearning for the paradise of infancy . . . [is] a quest that by definition has to fail' (Mermin, 1989, p. 194). 'There he stood, my king!' (VIII. 61), and thus arrives Romney. Once Aurora has admitted she loves Romney, she appears to lapse into a form of feminine deference at odds with her earlier principled independence. Romney holds a letter for Aurora from Lady

Waldemar, but dramatic suspense is strung out as the content is not revealed until Book IX. In the meantime Aurora and Romney communicate at cross purposes as Aurora assumes he is married.

Romney has read Aurora's book. It has made an impact: 'the book is in my heart, / Lives in me, wakes in me, and dreams me' (VIII. 265–6). Now he recognizes that poetry 'stands above my knowledge, draws me up' (VIII. 285–6) and says to Aurora 'never doubt that you're a poet [not poet*ess*] to me' (VIII. 591). Romney realizes poetry points to the ultimate truth, which is spiritual and not 'materialist' (VIII. 635). This is a more humble Romney than previously seen – he speaks of the 'disastrous arrogance' (VIII. 697) of his former views, and his dialogue is shot through with a not-quite-defined sense of failure. Aurora, by contrast, defends the 'earnest work / Of any honest creature, howbeit weak, / Imperfect, ill-adapted, fails so much' (VIII. 705–7), and, true to the Carlylean sentiments put into Aurora's mouth, recognizes Romney's efforts to 'give help' as 'heroic' (VIII. 786, 787). It is then revealed that Romney's socialistic endeavours have failed: 'my vain phalanstery dissolved itself' (VIII. 888). The message here is that it is not possible to force the renegade working classes to change for the better, as Leigh Hall's tenants burn down the homes Romney has created for them in a violent outpouring of antipathy towards upper-class philanthropy. The destruction of the ancestral home, with its symbolic burning of the entrenched patriarchy passed down with it, brings into focus one of the other 'intertexts' that haunts *Aurora Leigh*: *Jane Eyre* (1847).

The final lines of Book VIII reveal that Lady Waldemar is *not* actually Romney's wife and he passes Aurora the letter. Lady Waldemar redeems herself slightly: having diligently tended Romney through his illness and fevered ramblings about loving someone else, she then quietly removes herself from the scene. Perhaps her most genuine words are when she apologizes sincerely for what happened to Marian: 'I had sooner cut / My hand off . . . / Than crush her silly head with so much wrong' (IX. 98–9, 101). So . . . Romney is not married . . . but he is in Florence to claim *Marian* as his wife: 'As God sees things, I have a wife and child' (IX. 179). Marian says she will be 'bound' (IX. 246) by Aurora's guidance whether to accept him, and Aurora, with calm self-abnegation, gives them her blessing. The unfortunate animal analogies for Marian reappear en masse at this point, as her 'broad wild woodland eyes shot out a light', and she drops her 'impassioned spaniel head . . . On Romney's feet' (IX. 274, 277, 279). She escapes his embrace like a 'leaping fawn' (IX. 288). Yet another melodramatic twist is introduced as Marian then declares with dignity that she cannot marry Romney and that she 'Ha[s] come to learn, – a woman . . . / Despised or honoured, is a human soul, / And what her soul is, that she is herself' (IX. 328–30). Marian is suitably self-sacrificial, turned into a doting mother whose motherhood redeems the taint of fallenness. It is ultimately not clear what happens to her, as she then vanishes (IX. 452) from the poem. As with so many novelistic representations of the fallen woman, there is no realized reintegration into society. While she is not overtly punished she is denied the kind of fulfilment effectively handed over to Aurora.

Perhaps the most difficult plot revelation to swallow comes half way through Book IX. At the same moment Romney finally tells Aurora 'O love, I have loved you! O my soul . . .' (IX. 497), it is revealed that he is blind. Neither Aurora or Marian have noticed this for the past 1500 lines (although it is hinted at in VIII. 1091–3). Once again there are clear parallels to the ending of *Jane Eyre*. So the man Aurora ultimately accepts as an equal, appropriate partner for all her passionate artistry is both broken and blinded. If this seems harsh Mermin suggests that 'his blindness is a part of the thoroughgoing destruction of all forms of male power that he represents' (Mermin, 1989, p. 214). To hammer home yet more moral poetic justice to Romney for having been foolish enough to want to change the working classes, *and* for not marrying Marian, his blindness was partly caused by a falling beam in Leigh Hall as it was ablaze, seemingly 'tilt[ed] . . . my way' (IX. 557) by William Erle, Marian's no-good poacher of a father. Barrett Browning wrote about the blinding of Romney in a letter to Anna Jameson in 1856 and it was clearly intentional to make him lose his natural sight in order that he gain *in*sight.

Finally comes Aurora's declaration of love for Romney, along with her revised understanding that 'Art is much, but Love is more' (IX. 656). Gilbert and Gubar argue that this ending offers 'the most reasonable compromise between assertion and submission that a sane and worldly woman poet could achieve in the nineteenth century' (Gilbert and Gubar, 1979, p. 575). Their ecstatic long-withheld sexual consummation – a kiss – is figured in as passionate language as

Barrett Browning can muster, amidst 'convulsion[s]' and 'shuddering breaths' (IX. 721, 723).

Aurora Leigh ends with a utopian vision of the new union of man and woman working together to bring about a better world. The biblical book of Revelation's notion of the jewelled city of heaven – a new Jerusalem – is used to image this. Love wins the day, over Romney's former guides Fourier, Comte and Cabet, whom he now regards as 'void' and 'absurd' (IX. 868–9). Love wins because it is ultimately a mirror of the Love that is God. The earlier discussions of art versus work are now transmuted into a celebration of work and love. Significantly, Romney and Aurora's gendered roles are reversed when he asks her to 'work for two, / As I, though thus restrained, for two shall love!' (IX. 911–12).

Whether this somewhat mystical finale to *Aurora Leigh* is a genuine solution to Victorian class conflict is debatable. Arguably the work offers no real response and suggests instead that all efforts to improve the lot of the working classes by anyone of a higher class will fail because the working classes themselves do not want to change. It will take another thirty years for a socialism to emerge that is more genuinely rooted (post Marx) in the working class itself. Perhaps, as Aurora herself repeatedly suggests in relation to the transformatory possibilities of poetry, *Aurora Leigh* is less about offering pragmatic social blueprints than inspiring its readers to a greater and 'higher' vision of a society where gender relations above all else have been successfully reordered. Such a transformation will have implications not only for the future of poetry, but also for the way women and their sexuality are understood.

Reading

Avery, Simon (2011), *Elizabeth Barrett Browning.* Tavistock: Northcote House.

Avery, Simon and Rebecca Stott (2003), *Elizabeth Barrett Browning.* London: Longman.

Kaplan, Cora (1978), 'Introduction' to *Aurora Leigh, and Other Poems*, pp. 5–36. London: The Women's Press.

Mermin, Dorothy (1989), *Elizabeth Barrett Browning: The Origins of a New Poetry.* Chicago, IL: University of Chicago Press.

Research

- Reread Book 1.832–1026. What are some of the things Aurora claims for poetry, and how do they impact on her early writing?

- Reread Book V.139–222. In what ways does Aurora assert the continuing relevance of epic and poetry for her contemporary moment?

- Discuss *Aurora Leigh's* responses to (a) the fallen woman; (b) gender complementarity; (c) class division.

- How is reading *Aurora Leigh* different from reading a Victorian novel? How did *Aurora Leigh* being poetry impact on your reading?

6

Christina Rossetti, 'Goblin Market'

Christina Rossetti: Furniture wrecker

My favourite Pre-Raphaelite drawing shows Christina Rossetti smashing up the drawing room in apparent rage at reviews of her first published volume, *Goblin Market, and Other Poems* (1862, Wightwick Manor). The caricature's appeal lies in the incongruity between Christina Rossetti the reclusive, modest, devout Anglo-Catholic who sought (in the title of one of her poems) the 'lowest place', and the Christina Rossetti portrayed who is energetically taking a hammer to the furniture. The sketch is by brother Dante Gabriel, who also made several other drawings and paintings of her. All depict the more sanguine, serious Christina, and she figures as the model for the young Virgin Mary in two of his defining Pre-Raphaelite paintings, *The Girlhood of Mary Virgin* (1848–9, Tate Britain) and *Ecce Ancilla Domini! (The Annunciation)* (1849, Tate Britain).

While Rossetti cultivated a certain self-effacing persona in her life, driven by her Christian beliefs, she also had a quietly determined commitment to her poetry. Rossetti's sense of herself as a poet is very different to that of Barrett Browning: whereas the latter consciously took on the male Romantic tradition and addressed contemporary issues via the form of epic, Rossetti's lyrical voice – teasing, mystical, playful, lovelorn, melancholic and richly sensuous – constantly negotiates between public and private. In some of her short lyrics the voice speaks from an 'after death' perspective or invites the reader to remember her once dead ('Remember'; 'Song: When I am dead, my dearest'; 'At Home'). Rossetti lived with a strong awareness of death, not least because of various ailments that inflicted her as an adult, including the disfiguring Graves disease; this awareness was compounded by her devout theology. She is also sometimes associated with the poetic expression of an intense 'hope deferred' ('The heart knoweth its own bitterness', 49; 'Three Stages', 2) which blurs boundaries between sexual and religious desire:

> I long for one to stir my deep –
>   I have had enough of help and gift –
>   I long for one to search and sift
> Myself, to take myself and keep.   ('The heart knoweth', 29–32)

Rossetti 'arrived' as a poet in the 1860s and as such represented a new and changing poetry aesthetic which made Barrett Browning and Tennyson increasingly look like the 'old'. It may seem surprising to mention Rossetti in the same sentence as the atheistic Swinburne, whose *Poems and Ballads* (1866) caused scandal and deflected critical attention away from Rossetti's first volume, but they were both 'in the vanguard of the transition from the mid- to the dominant late-Victorian poetic mode, with its intense but dreamlike imaginative world' (Marsh, 1995, p. 358).

Indeed Swinburne and many other contemporaries regarded Rossetti as one of the finest living poets of her day. Lewis Carroll, whose innovations with the possibilities of nonsense can be compared to Rossetti's own in *Sing-Song* (1872), wished her to be considered for Poet Laureate on Tennyson's death in 1892. However, Amy Sharp's 1891 account of Victorian poets gives Barrett Browning an entire chapter but consigns Rossetti to a crowded 'Minor Poets' chapter at the back. But by 1923 Marjorie Bald's study of *Women Writers of the Nineteenth Century* very clearly favours Rossetti over Barrett Browning:

> For sheer intensity there is . . . no comparison between the two women. Christina's soul was like a radiant texture, its colours flashing and quivering as if some hidden life were rippling through

its folds. Mrs Browning's soul was of the same colour, but in a
paler shade, and woven of plainer threads.   (Bald, 1923, p. 251)

Rossetti could also 'hold her lips firmly closed', unlike her 'garrulous'
foremother (p. 247), but Bald nevertheless concludes that 'She is
not now, and probably never will be, widely popular' (p. 267). This
couldn't be more wrong. Despite her considerable œuvre of religious
poetry, and the devotional writings that made Rossetti more money
in her life than her poetry ever did (*Seek and Find* [1879], *Called to
be Saints* [1881], *Letter and Spirit* [1883], *Time Flies: A Reading Diary*
[1885]), even then 'Goblin Market' was 'her best known poem . . .
the happiest possible combination of serious fancy and mirthful earnest' (Sharp, 1891, pp. 189–90).

  In a nod towards Rossetti's 1885 'Reading Diary' Isobel Armstrong
writes her own diary essay on how, 'during public examinations and
throughout my undergraduate career no single poem by Christina
Rossetti was put before us for close reading' (Armstrong, 1987,
p. 119). Armstrong notes how the Pelican Guides to English Literature
of the 1950s consolidated the view (after F. R. Leavis) that what
constituted 'The Great Tradition' (1950) of Victorian literature was
the novel. While this marginalized all Victorian poetry, women poets
were doubly disadvantaged. Poetry is however discussed in the
Pelican Guide on the Victorians and again Rossetti is given more
space than Barrett Browning, but Armstrong notes that the critics
had no real way of dealing with what they regarded as her 'simplic-
ity' (Armstrong, 1987, p. 119). What were they to do with 'Christina
Rossetti, who as a violent child slashed her arm with scissors,
[and] who as an adult wrote "Goblin Market" (not discussed in the
Guide), a poem so scandalous that it could only be read by children'
(p. 122).

Giving and withholding:
'Winter: My Secret'

Rossetti's poetry still appeals because 'her work deliberately culti-
vates uncertainty and enigma; it is slippery and elusive, sometimes

flagrantly refusing to offer stability of meaning' (Burlinson, 1998, p. 1).
This is exemplified in a poem such as 'Winter: My Secret' (1862):

> I tell my secret? No indeed, not I!
> Perhaps some day, who knows?
> But not today; it froze, and blows, and snows,
> And you're too curious: fie!
> You want to hear it? well:
> Only my secret's mine, and I won't tell.
>
> Or, after all, perhaps there's none:
> Suppose there is no secret after all,
> But only just my fun.   (1–9)

The teasing voice here both gives and withholds – a characteristic
Rossetti trait. The poem's opening suggests there *is* a secret to be
discovered, but by line seven this is called into playful question. It
also demonstrates Rossetti's skill in varying pace through lines of differing metrical length, and her love of repetition and word-play. The
repetition of sound in poetry is, of course, the basis of rhyme, but the
more similar sounds repeat, the more words empty of meaning and
the sound of the poetry itself starts to take precedence over sense.
The manuscript version of this poem was originally titled 'Nonsense',
interestingly enough; but is this poem mere nonsense?

> Today's a nipping day, a biting day;
> In which one wants a shawl,
> A veil, a cloak, and other wraps:
> I cannot ope to every one who taps,
> And let the draughts come whistling thro' my hall;
> Come bounding and surrounding me,
> Come buffeting, astounding me,
> Nipping and clipping thro' my wraps and all.   (10–17)

Note Rossetti's use of half rhymes and internal rhymes here: the
assonance of 'n*i*pping' becomes 'b*i*ting', 'veil' echoes 'shawl', 'ope'
echoes 'wraps' and 'taps'. The bounding winter draughts which
assail the speaker may remind us of Lizzie being assailed by the
goblins when they are 'No longer wagging, purring, / But visibly

demurring, / Grunting and snarling' (391–3). The change of title to map the season of winter onto the poem's sense of secrecy doesn't actually help explain what the secret might be, but the seasons add a rich metaphoric layer. Interestingly spring is no more likely a time for the revelation of secrets than winter here – 'I don't trust / March with its peck of dust' (23–4). It is in the fullness of summer, when 'golden fruit is ripening to excess' (30) that the speaker comes closest to suggesting that 'Perhaps' (28, 33) the secret might be told, 'Or you may guess' (34). As Kathyrn Burlinson says, 'What is notable in Rossetti's handling of the topic [of secrets] is her refusal to provide readers with the pleasurable satisfaction of having discovered the secret' (Burlinson, 1998, p. 18). 'I wear my mask for warmth' (18) says the speaker: concealment is all.

Critical approaches to 'Goblin Market'

The amount of criticism on 'Goblin Market' is somewhat daunting, with nuance upon nuance of each new reading superseding the last. Reviewing Rossetti's first volume in 1863 Caroline Norton asked of the title poem 'Is it a fable – or a mere fairy story – or an allegory against the pleasures of sinful love – or what is it?' (Burlinson, 1998, p. 7). The desire to fix the meaning of this poem has been there from the outset, yet Norton's final question – 'what is it?' – seems very like one of the teasing questions Rossetti poses to her readers in several of her poems, and ultimately there is no definitive answer. Pressed for some kind of interpretive finality herself Rossetti claimed that 'Goblin Market' was a mere fairy story for children, without 'any profound or ulterior meaning' (Bell, 1898, p. 230). This has done nothing to arrest the avalanche of often very adult readings which have appeared since renewed attention has been given to Rossetti from the 1970s onwards. The remainder of this chapter will approach the poem by way of a critical survey of just a small selection of the many readings available. In itself this exercise will demonstrate the very diversity of possible approaches that can be taken in relation to Victorian poetry.

In *The Madwoman in the Attic* (1979), Gilbert and Gubar's discussion of 'Goblin Market' comes in a chapter on women poets with the subtitle 'The Aesthetics of Renunciation'. They suggest that 'the conscious or semi-conscious allegorical intention of this narrative poem is sexual/religious' (Gilbert and Gubar, 1979, p. 566): the fruits that the goblin men offer the two sisters are clearly sexual in such a reading. Lizzie (the 'good' girl) says 'You should not peep at goblin men' (49) to Laura (the 'bad' girl), who knows she shouldn't 'linger' (69) but who nonetheless still buys of the goblins' fruits with a 'golden curl' (125). Having paid with the only currency available to middle-class Victorian women – her body – Laura crosses the line from domestic idyll of innocence to the fallen decline of experience. Numerous inter-texts cry for attention here, including the biblical account of Eve's eating of the fruit of the tree of knowledge in Genesis, John Milton's *Paradise Lost* (1667) and Alexander Pope's *The Rape of the Lock* (1714). Following the biblical scheme of fall and redemption, Gilbert and Gubar note that Lizzie functions as a salvific Christ(a) figure, who 'rehabilitates Laura, changing her back from a lost witch to a virginal bride, and ultimately leading her into a heaven of innocent domesticity' (p. 566). They read the final epilogue to the poem (lines 543–67) negatively, as a retreat into a 'virginal female world . . . rejecting any notions of sexuality, of self-assertion, of personal pleasure' (p. 567). But as many fallen women do not achieve reintegration into any kind of future in Victorian texts it could be argued that the reconstituted idyll here is still a radical gesture. Gilbert and Gubar also note that the ending valorizes the powerful possibilities of sisterhood ("For there is no friend like a sister", 562) – in a contemporary feminist use of the word. They thus pave the way for many subsequent readings which focus on the 'strikingly sexual redemption scene between the sisters' which leaves us at the end with a 'covertly (if ambivalently) lesbian world' (p. 567) in which men don't feature. Mary Wilson Carpenter, for example, suggests that 'the poem not only affirms the female body and its appetites but constructs "sisterhood" as a saving female homoerotic bond' (Carpenter, 1991, p. 417). A more overtly queer take on the poem's most sexually-charged scene, when Laura invites Lizzie to 'Come and kiss me. / Never mind the bruises, / Hug me, kiss me, suck my juices' (466–68), is far more explicit: 'If reading "Goblin Market" as lesbian s/m porn is wrong', says Heather Love, 'I don't want to be right' (Love, 2007, p. 161). An alternative queer reading might ask whether the poem's 'extraordinary homoerotic energies' (Carpenter, 1991, p. 417) solely concern the sisters; after all, Laura is attracted to, and Lizzie has to resist 'Brother and queer brother' (94).

Reading biographically, Jan Marsh sets her consideration of the poem after discussion of Rossetti's voluntary work at St Mary Magdalene Penitentiary in Highgate, north London, begun in 1859. 'Goblin Market' was finished in April of the same year, and Marsh suggests that it 'seems very probable that [it] was conceived as an engaging but moral tale for the Penitentiary' (Marsh, 1995, p. 235). It is certainly possible to read the poem as a cautionary tale for young Victorian women about the temptations and dangers of male sexuality, particularly if those women have already been designated 'fallen'. While Marsh is careful to say that 'erotic readings of "Goblin Market" are our creations, not Christina's' (Marsh, 1995, p. 232) she still reads several key passages of the poem as highly sexualized and is far from the first to regard the goblins' violent attempts to force Lizzie to taste their fruits as a kind of rape:

> They trod and hustled her,
> Elbowed and jostled her,
> Clawed with their nails,
> Barking, mewing, hissing, mocking,
> Tore her gown and soiled her stocking . . .   (399–403)

The 'juice that syrupped all [Lizzie's] face' (434) here becomes 'an image of ejaculation' (p. 233).

If it is practically impossible not to read the poem as somehow concerning female sexuality, critics have also noted that 'Goblin Market' is – as its title says – about the *market* and a world of economic exchange (see Holt, 1991). The goblins are 'merchant m[e]n' (70) and their siren-song is 'Come buy, come buy'. The fruits aren't gifts; they have to be bought. But the goblins' market actually operates a means of exchange that isn't about money: Laura has no copper or silver in her purse (118–19) and although Lizzie offers a coin the goblins 'Fl[i]ng back her penny' (439). There are alternative means of exchange that the goblins prefer – 'Buy from us with a golden curl' (125) – and what riles them about Lizzie is not whether she can pay but rather that she does not want to taste the juices of their fruits: she 'Would not open lip from lip / Lest they should cram a mouthful in' (431–2). As Elizabeth Helsinger notes, Lizzie 're-establish[es] a necessary separation between acts of economic exchange and the expression of desire. She buys but does not consume' (Helsinger, 1991, p. 924). Helsinger's reading ultimately suggests that Victorian women 'must enter a marketplace in which they are always at risk' (p. 926) and their successful negotiation of such a sexual economy is dependent on their 'reclaim[ing] the power of money as their own' (ibid.) and 'the mutual support of women for women' (ibid.).

Critics have also read the poem in relation to various historical contexts. Mary Arseneau focuses on the influence of Tractarianism (the Oxford Movement) on Rossetti and reads Lizzie's sacrificial exposure to the goblins' fruits as an 'Eucharistic offering of herself' (Arseneau, 1993, p. 90). Diane D'Amico also reads the poem in the light of Rossetti's faith and alongside her other devotional writings. In this context Lizzie and Laura's climactic scene is redemptive and 'an affirmation of the power of the spiritual over the sensual' (D'Amico, 1999, p. 78). In a poem with such a sensuous list of fruits as an integral part of its opening section and which is all about the plea-sures and perils of tasting and sucking, many readings focus on food. Rebecca Stern raises concerns about food adulteration in the late 1850s (Stern, 2003), while Richard Menke notes that serious frosts in the spring of 1859 may well have affected the availability of fruit crops later in the year, alongside fruit becoming more widely avail-able and less of a luxury during the nineteenth century (Menke, 1999, pp. 108–9). Anna Krugovoy Silver reminds us that anorexia nervosa was first diagnosed by physicians in 1873 and also that 'the repres-sion of worldiness, particularly appetite, is a theme that runs through Rossetti's work'. The doubling of Laura and Lizzie can be read as 'an anorexic paradigm . . . Lizzie thus epitomizes the laudable refusal to eat, whereas Laura, by devouring huge amounts of food, stands for the desire to binge' (Silver, 2002, pp. 136, 140).

Picking up on the colonial contexts in which all Victorian writ-ing was produced, Menke also notes that the descriptions of the animal-like goblins include wombats (75), ratels (76) and parrots (112), all of which can be found in Britain's colonies. The suggestion that the goblins resemble animals both exotically foreign and domestic 'hint[s] at the dangers of intimacy and confusion between home and abroad' (Menke, 1999, p. 118). Krista Lysack mixes imperial and economic themes. She suggests that most economic readings have 'tended not to ensure a space for the production of female desire *within* market economies', but in the light of the development of the department store (such as Harrods and Liberty's) which offers women the *pleasure* of shopping, 'we begin to see the marketplace of Rossetti's poem not simply as a place of danger and temptation for women but also as a significant site for the formation of their identities and desires' (Lysack, 2008, p. 16). This reading isn't about sexuality, and Lysack regards the goblins, with their repeated cry of 'Come buy, come buy', as 'consummate ad-men for imperial capitalism whose job it is to hawk and even impose tempting delights' (p. 41).

Visualizing 'Goblin Market'

Rossetti's original manuscript title for the poem was 'A Peep at the Goblins' and this introduces one of the most interesting contexts in which to read the poem. From the very outset, in a poem all about the pleasures and perils of looking, the visual has had a place alongside the verbal. As Lorraine Janzen Kooistra has pointed out, 'from 1862 to the present, "Goblin Market" has sparked the imaginations of at least eighteen artists . . . from the Pre-Raphaelite to the postmodern' (Kooistra, 1999, p. 137). The very first of these was Christina's own brother: not only did Dante Gabriel suggest a change of title, but he also provided the title page and frontispiece illustrations to the first edition. This established a visual approach to the poem which has implicitly influenced every other illustrated edition since. The title-page image, which depicts Laura and Lizzie as two (D. G.) Rossettian 'stunners', asleep in each other's arms, is 'tinged with eroticism', and also sets the precedent for how 'illustrated editions of the poem tend to position the reader/viewer outside a picture frame in which Lizzie and Laura become passive objects of the gaze' (Kooistra, 1999, pp. 142, 143). In 1893 Laurence Housman, younger brother of poet A. E., also illustrated the poem, with twelve full-page pictures and lots of textual ornamentation. This slim volume, with its art nouveau cover, is one of the fin de siècle's most appealing illustrated volumes of poetry. Where Rossetti's focus was on the two sisters, Housman's is much more on the goblins. They have human, clothed bodies, but animal and bird heads. The depiction of the emergent sexuality of the sisters, and the potentially menacing goblins, has fascinated numerous illustrators (see Chapter 10).

Rossetti's irresistible metres

'Goblin Market' is undoubtedly a very appealing poem, but it is more than its content that seduces the reader. The poem's sensory over-load is compounded through its 'irresistible and innovative' (Marsh, 1994, p. 443) use of varying lengths of metrical lines. Dante Gabriel sent some of Christina's poems to John Ruskin in 1861 and the lat-ter's feedback was that they would never get published because they were full of 'irregular measure . . . the calamity of modern poetry' (cited in Menke, 1999, p. 123). But the messing up of metri-cal smoothness we find in 'Goblin Market' is now to us not a sign of its failure but quite the opposite. The poem's opening section of thirty-one lines is written with a strong two beats per line, mostly in a thumping dactylic (/ x x) metre:

> Morning and evening
> Maids heard the goblins cry:
> 'Come buy our orchard fruits,
> Come buy, come buy . . .   (1–4)

Although overall the underlying metrical foot of the poem is beat-offbeat(s) many lines play about with this, sometimes reversing to iambics (x /), and in some sections lines contain varying numbers of feet:

>   x / x / (2)
> She ran and ran
>   x / x /   x   / x   / (4)
> As if she feared some goblin man

```
  /    x   x   /   x   /   (3)
Dogged her with jibe or curse
x    /    x    /   (2)
Or something worse:
  x   /  x    /  x   /   x  / x   (4)
But not one goblin scurried after,
  /    x   x    /    x   /   (3)
Nor was she pricked by fear;
  x   /    x    /    x  /   x   /    (4)
The kind heart made her windy-paced
  x   /   x   /    x   /  x   /    x    /   (5)
That urged her home quite out of breath with haste
  x  /  x    /    x   (2)
And inward laughter.                              (455–63)
```

This keeps the reader on his or her toes: you never *quite* know what's coming next, by way of rhythm and rhyme. Angela Leighton writes that 'the whole energy and inspiration of the work drive towards more temptation, more fruit and more poetry' (Leighton, 1992, p. 138). It is a poem one doesn't want to end, which perhaps explains why the final more reflective section (lines 543–67) which reasserts a domestic setting can seem a disappointment. Whatever threat the goblins pose, there is an undoubted energy associated with them, and the poem's linguistic vitality communicates this. Steven Connor has suggested that 'the temptation to sin which the goblins represent is as much to indulge oneself in language, in a kind of verbal promiscuity, as in sexual or sensual abandon' (Connor, 1984, p. 444).

The poem's capacity both to encourage interpretive overload *and* also to resist anything like conclusive readings points to poetry's ability more generally (as crafted language made from sound and pulse and repetition) to evade being turned into anything other than itself. The reader trying to find her way through the market of readings of this poem could be forgiven for feeling a bit like Lizzie when she is assailed by the goblins' fruits: 'Look at our apples / Russet and dun, / Bob at our cherries, / Bite at our peaches' (352–5). As we all know, it then turns nasty, but ultimately Lizzie does not buy any of the fruits (and hence any of the myriad readings of the poem). She may be covered with the juice of a little bit of all of them, and that leaves her 'In a smart, ache, tingle' (447), but this is redemptive rather than any reason to be 'pricked by fear' (460). I am not arguing for dehistoricized readings or readings that remove 'Goblin Market' from continuing illuminating collisions with the numerous contexts that surround Rossetti's life and moment – far from it. But – to be as teasing as Rossetti herself – 'Goblin Market' still manages to remain as 'deliciously mystifying' (Menke, 1999, p. 129) after many reads as it is after the first. It will not be bought by the coin of literary criticism.

Reading

Arseneau, Mary, Antony H. Harrison and Lorraine Janzen Kooistra, eds (1999), *The Culture of Christina Rossetti: Female Poetics and Victorian Contexts*. Athens, GA: Ohio University Press.

Burlinson, Kathryn (1998), *Christina Rossetti*. Plymouth: Northcote House.

Chapman, Alison (2000), *The Afterlife of Christina Rossetti*. Basingstoke: Macmillan.

Kooistra, Lorraine Janzen (2002), *Christina Rossetti and Illustration: A Publishing History*. Athens, OH: Ohio University Press.

Marsh, Jan (1995 [1994]), *Christina Rossetti: A Literary Biography*. London: Pimlico.

Research

● Offer a reading of one of Rossetti's poems that demonstrates how her poetry both gives and withholds.

● Using a bibliographic database such as the Modern Language Association (MLA) bibliography, or the Criticism section of LION (Literature Online), find an article that offers a reading of 'Goblin Market'. Using an online discussion forum, summarize the article's argument and post it for your classmates to see. What do you make of the many differing responses to this poem?

● Search out one of the many illustrated editions that have engaged with the poem since 1862. Focussing on one illustration, what lines in the poem does it illustrate? How is the illustration interpreting the poem?

7

Dante Gabriel Rossetti, 'Jenny' and Augusta Webster, 'A Castaway'

'Jenny': The one most wanted

'Jenny' was begun in 1847–8 and revised heavily in the late 1850s. The poem is implicated in the most notorious story known about Rossetti: when his wife, Elizabeth Siddall, died of a laudanum overdose in 1862, the sole manuscript of his unpublished poems went into the grave with her. In the late 1860s Rossetti wished to publish, so the coffin was reopened to recover the manuscript. The report of the exhumation is given in letters to brother William Michael and fellow painter Ford Madox Brown in October 1869. Rossetti refers intriguingly to the coffin being found 'quite perfect', but tells Brown there is 'a great hole right through all the leaves of "Jenny" which was the thing I most wanted'. In a letter to William Michael, Rossetti adds a sketch of the manuscript with the worm-hole drawn in (Fredeman, 2004, pp. 303, 304).

This notion of 'Jenny' the poem, but also the figure of Jenny the prostitute, as being the most wanted is suggestive. The poem is one of Rossetti's finest, and it is clear from his letters that he cared a great deal about the reception of his first volume in 1870, despite being well established as a painter. 'Jenny' was considered 'shockingly explicit in its own day' (Michie, 1989, p. 61), and in the famous response to Richard Buchanan's notorious attack on his poetry as belonging to 'The Fleshly School', Rossetti states that he has long been aware of the 'charges of recklessness and aggressiveness' that might be levelled at him for considering such subject matter ('The Stealthy School of Criticism', 1871; McGann, 2003, p. 337). Rossetti's defence of 'Jenny' includes the suggestion that 'the motive powers of art . . . demand first of all an *inner* standing point' which Jerome McGann glosses as 'a neglected but major contribution to the theory of art and poetry' (McGann, 2003, pp. 337, 411). Rossetti continues:

> The heart of such a mystery as this [why any woman would become a prostitute] must be plucked from the very world in which it beats or bleeds; and the beauty and pity, the self-questionings and all-questionings which it brings with it, can come with full force only from the mouth of one alive to its whole appeal, such as the speaker put forward in the poem – that is, of a young and thoughtful man of the world.   (McGann, 2003, pp. 337–8)

This is an interesting justification of the necessary aestheticization of the prostitute in order that she may be considered aright. It is also an argument for the poem's perspective: the only voice that can speak of the prostitute's 'beauty and pity' is the liberal male voice of 'Jenny'.

As with many monologues there is an implied dramatic scenario. Our 'speaker' is an intelligent, cultured man who has exchanged his room 'so full of books' (23) for Jenny's room – possibly a hired room in a brothel. He has danced the night away with

> Lazy laughing languid Jenny,
> Fond of a kiss and fond of a guinea,
> Whose head upon my knee to-night
> Rests for a while, as if grown light
> With all our dances and the sound
> To which the wild tunes spun you round . . .   (1–6)

The fact that Jenny has fallen asleep before any sexual encounter has taken place is integral to the poem's structure: it is precisely because the sexual transaction (I use an economic term deliberately) doesn't happen that our speaker is forced to ruminate on Jenny as prostitute and how he too is implicated. These opening lines set the scene *and* do a lot of poetic work: from line three onwards the underlying metric pattern of iambic tetrameter couplets is established (although on sixteen occasions, three lines rhyme together). But the first two lines reverse the iambs to trochees so the initial line scans / x / x / x / x. Line three adds in a couple of dactyls with their extra off-beat (/ x x / x / x x / x) to emphasize the parallelism of the line that links kisses and guineas as things Jenny is 'fond of' (known as a zeugma). Sound also forces associations: 'Jenny' is linked to the half rhyme of 'guinea' and the repeating 'stressed-unstressed' pattern of the opening three 'I' words – all adjectives to describe Jenny – make for a memorable opening line. Iambic tetrameter couplets offer a lively rhythmic and metrical pattern and they work well in long(ish) narrative poems (see also Morris's 'The Haystack in the Floods'). There is also much use of enjambment throughout, as the speaking voice often over-rides the end of lines.

A key question is what the reader makes of the speaker. He is 'a liberal male intellectual, someone who in the nineteenth-century humanist tradition would have prided himself on open-mindedness, sensitivity, tolerance and moral idealism' (Slinn, 2003, p. 129). The poet presents his nonchalant, colloquial tone: 'Well, I suppose 'twas hard to part, / For here I am. And now, sweetheart, / You seem too tired to get to bed' (34–6). Considering he doesn't get what he came to Jenny's room for, he imagines she may be 'glad / That I'm not drunk or ruffianly / And let you rest upon my knee' (64–6). He treats her much better than some, it's implied. But our speaker is caught time and again between desire and repulsion. He romanticizes and aestheticizes Jenny, turning her into one of the women in a Rossetti painting:

> Why Jenny as I watch you there, –
> For all your wealth of loosened hair,
> Your silk ungirdled and unlac'd
> And warm sweets open to the waist . . .   (46–9)

She is beautiful, but one of the poem's repeated concerns is the difficulty of telling the sexually unrespectable woman from the respectable. Almost from the outset our speaker says Jenny is a 'Fresh flower, scarce touched with signs that tell / Of Love's exuberant hotbed' (12–13). There's a sense of amazement: she doesn't *look* like a prostitute, as though her sexual behaviour should write itself onto her body. But straightaway our speaker turns to an opposite image: 'Poor flower left torn since yesterday' and 'Poor handful of bright spring-water / Flung in the whirlpool's shrieking face' (14, 16–17). She sleeps 'Just as another woman sleeps!' (177; note the exclamation mark). The impossibility of telling the virtuous from the impure woman is 'Enough to throw one's thoughts in heaps / Of doubt and horror' (178–9). Even though he wants to be sympathetic and is beguiled by Jenny's beauty he also cannot escape the discourses which condemn the transgressive woman: 'is there hue or shape defin'd / In Jenny's desecrated mind, / Where all contagious currents meet . . . [?]' (163–5). Jenny embodies the paradoxical double-bind of male attitudes to female sexuality in the Victorian period: she is 'Poor shameful Jenny, full of grace' (18) and 'So pure, – so fall'n!' (207). Our speaker's cousin Nell is 'fond of fun' (185), just like Jenny, and also 'fond of dress, and change, and praise' (186), just like Jenny. There are only two lines in the whole poem that are set on their own and the first is the speaker's response to the disturbing conundrum of both Nell and Jenny being 'Of the same lump . . . [of clay] / For honour and dishonour made' (183–4); and in what seems to be an allusion to sister Christina's famous poem, this 'makes a goblin of the sun' (206).

Jenny's silence

Dante Gabriel counselled his sister against including a poem about an unmarried mother and her illegitimate child ('Under the Rose') in her new volume, as he thought the subject 'might not be suitable for a woman' (Leighton, 1989, p. 115). Rossetti's counsel suggests another of the questions which permeate 'Jenny': who can speak for the fallen woman? In one of the poem's extended similes the speaker likens her to 'a rose shut in a book / In which pure women may not look' (253–4), suggesting that Jenny's 'shameful knowledge' (265) will contaminate through association if 'chaste' (266) women take an interest in her. The problem some readers have with this poem is that our male speaker does literally *speak for* Jenny. She has no voice at all. The imagining of her life and her thoughts is entirely filtered through a male consciousness. This can be taken further if we consider that this is actually a monologue in which the speaker *doesn't speak*. Daniel Harris has described 'Jenny' as 'the first interior monologue in English Literary tradition' (Harris, 1984, p. 197). Our liberal gentleman has left his books behind and doesn't want to think, but because Jenny falls asleep (and she seems very determined to – see lines 89–95) he is forced to do far more thinking than expected: 'do not let me think of you / Lest shame of yours suffice for two' (91–2). What the monologue thus consists of is 'the speaker's very articulate thought process' (Slinn, 2003, p. 131). Despite the dramatic asides to try and keep her awake the point is actually that she must stay asleep and he must not speak directly to her. 'Suppose I were to think aloud, – / What if to her all this were said?' (156–7) is a key question. As Harris has noted, if she did hear what he was saying she might well respond and this could challenge the construction of 'Jenny' that we are given. There is also a potential inequity between the speaker and the implied auditor in a monologue, and in 'Jenny' 'this particularly suits a poem about the imbalances of sexual power' (Harris, 1984, p. 202). Because she is asleep Jenny is an utterly passive object for the male gaze, which turns her into art with every progressing line. He notes how 'Jenny's long throat droops aside, – / The shadows where the cheeks are thin, / And pure wide curve from ear to chin . . .' (234–6). Our speaker provocatively asks why Jenny's face could not be 'gilded' with an 'aureole' by such as 'Raffael' or 'Leonardo' in a painting used for religious instruction and adoration (230–40). But praising her beauty is no substitute for the fact that 'Victorian discourses characteristically construct the prostitute as one who lacks agency' (Anderson, 1993, p. 7). In aestheticizing Jenny the painterly eye of our speaker ceases to see her as an actual woman and turns her into Woman.

Even if this is an interior monologue, it is also very much a *dramatic* monologue. The poem uses its dramatic scene to occasion the very necessity of the monologue itself, and then enacts the passing of the night the speaker spends with Jenny asleep on his knee. At the point when our speaker looks as though he would now like some action, following a rumination on the eternal toadness of 'Lust' (247), it is too late: 'Jenny, wake up . . . Why, there's the dawn!' (303).

The prostitute and art: 'Jenny' and *Found*

The coming of the new morning also draws the reader's attention to 'an early waggon drawn / To market, and some sheep that jog / Bleating before a barking dog' (304–6). This links the poem to Rossetti's unfinished painting *Found* (begun 1854), which features a drover bringing a tethered lamb to the city for slaughter, who encounters a former sweetheart who has now become a prostitute. She turns her head away from him into the wall she has been sleeping beside, ashamed to have been so 'found'. Rossetti started drafting studies for *Found* in the early 1850s and the numerous studies he made for it can be seen in the online Rossetti Archive. The most complete versions of the picture are two almost identical pen and ink drawings of 1853 (British Museum; Gere, 1994, p. 25) and c. 1854–5 (Birmingham; Wildman, 1995, p. 145). In the incomplete painting the phallic short tethering post looms up wonkily out of the blank unfinished ground. The images also make clear who is at the centre of Rossetti's response to this subject and thus sit uneasily alongside 'Jenny' as a response to a prostitute which is really about male subjectivity and deflected desire. If Jenny isn't able to be seduced fully in the poem then perhaps it is the *reader* who is to be seduced into thinking that *this* is the right view of the fallen woman. Our gentleman doesn't force himself on Jenny physically, but Jenny has no choice in being turned into an art object. Even the hard cash transactional nature of our speaker still paying Jenny by laying golden coins in her golden hair is turned into a fantasized moment of beauty as he imagines her waking and 'shak[ing] / My gold, in rising, from your hair, / A Danaë for a moment there' (377–9). Is this thus actually a poem about an aesthetic rape?

Our speaker doesn't appear to get what he came for, but still

> I lay among your golden hair,
> Perhaps the subject of your dreams,
> These golden coins.   (340–2)

Line 342 is the *only* broken line in the entire poem. It is a literal 'money shot', in every sense of that phrase, and the climax of the poem. But as we have seen before, sexual desire is often closely followed by revulsion: it is hard not to see the sexual connotations of Jenny having a 'magic purse' (344), but straightaway our speaker almost spits out his disgust as he describes it as a 'Grim web, how clogged with shrivelled flies!' (345). Death lurks at the edges of every image of beauty offered . . . how fitting that a worm gnawed its way through the poem in the buried manuscript. In the drawings for *Found* the woman turns her face away to the wall of a graveyard.

Despite never finishing *Found* Rossetti nonetheless wrote a poem for it (published 1881) – one of the many 'double works' which involve his writing a poem (often a sonnet) to accompany a painting. In 'Found (For a Picture)' the poem asks of the prostitute's plight, 'Can day from darkness ever again take flight?' (8). This is the question that haunts so many representations of the fallen woman, where social reintegration is debarred. '[R]esurrection' (4) may be hinted at, but is rarely enacted. Instead, what must *always* be produced and made manifest is the fallen woman's sense of shame. Versions of the word 'shame' are repeated eight times in 'Jenny', but because Jenny remains asleep she is incapable of manifesting the necessary shame, so our speaker can only impute it to her. Jenny's 'shameful knowledge' (265) must not be witnessed by other women for fear that they might want it too. Shame is notoriously contagious, and Jenny's silence means that our speaker is unable to escape contamination; ultimately he is 'Ashamed of [his] own shame' (384). We are left with the possibility that our speaker has learnt something through this night of thinking and not acting: 'By a far gleam which I may near, / A dark path I can strive to clear' (389–90). But note the lack of certainty in *may*, and the vagueness of *far gleam*.

What is it about this subject matter that meant Rossetti returned to it obsessively in works like 'Jenny' and *Found*? The two pen and ink drawings are practically identical – neither shows substantial development from the other. With the painting in particular there is an anxiety manifest in Rossetti's reworking and reworking it but never actually being able to finish. Joseph Bristow notes Rossetti's 'ambivalen[ce] about whether these poems should occupy the private or the public sphere' (Bristow, 1993, pp. 100–1) and how Rossetti himself saw the necessity of engaging with 'the market' as prostituting his art. Bristow suggests that 'not only the scholarly young man but also Rossetti's poem . . . wish to protect themselves from the kinds of humiliation that the streetwalker suffers at the hands of the public' (p. 106). To what extent your sympathy in reading this poem is with our paradoxically silent speaker is for you to decide.

Augusta Webster: Dramatic monologist

Augusta Webster (1837–94) has been rediscovered as one of the finest Victorian writers of dramatic monologues. In the 1860s Webster became involved in the emerging suffrage movement and she 'belongs in the liberal, humanitarian tradition of the high Victorians, with its social responsibility and philanthropical concerns' (Leighton, 1992, pp. 166–7). In the later 1870s Webster wrote journalistic articles for the *Examiner*, collected together as *A Housewife's Opinions* (1879). Essays concerned with women's experiences ranged from discussions of higher education to working conditions to the extension of the franchise to husband hunting. Another essay, 'Poets and Personal Pronouns' (1878), takes on the naïve reader of poetry who conflates poet and speaker whenever a poet writes 'I', and suggests that poets need to create vividly realized characters as much as any novelist. This is an important point for a Victorian woman poet to make and legitimates Webster's own poetic practice in her use of the monologue form in *Dramatic Studies* (1866), *A Woman Sold* (1867) and *Portraits* (1870). As Glennis Byron has noted, in a cultural and literary context which

> . . . linked women with the private and men with the public, there was a tendency to associate women writers with the personal and confessional . . . Speaking in the voice of a dramatized 'I' is a way of insisting that . . . her work *is* art, not simply an outpouring of personal feeling.   (Byron, 2003, pp. 46–7)

Leighton has noted Webster's crucial difference from the Browning model of dramatic monologue:

> [Her] speakers are not so much victims of an irony which exposes their double standards . . . as they are victims of historical and social double standards outside themselves. Especially when those

speakers are women, the element of morbid criminality . . . gives way to more ordinary inconsistencies of the self, as it gazes in the mirror of external expectations and ideals.   (Leighton, 1992, p. 178)

Webster's speakers are ordinary men and women who explore the social constraints within which they find themselves. Thus in 'By the Looking Glass' (1866) a young woman with 'so plain a face!' (17) escapes from the painful self-consciousness of a ball to muse alone on how she lost the man she loved to her 'young fair sister bright with her bloom' (178). In 'The Happiest Girl in the World' (1870) the newly-engaged speaker reveals an anxious gap between the fantasy of romance and the actual reality: 'oh to think he should be loving me / And I be no more moved out of myself!' (80–81). In 'Faded' (1893) a single woman ruminates in front of a mirror that she is losing her looks, and explores the implications of this as she grows older: 'The first dead leaves are falling and all's past. / Myself has faded from me; I am old' (35–6). In 'Tired' (1870) a husband reflects on his part in turning an 'artless girl, come from her cottage home' (26) into an 'artificial' (165), fashionable, trophy wife: 'She is just a bird / Born in a wicker cage and brought away / Into a gilded one . . . unconceiving freedom, [she] chirrups on, / Content to see her prison bars so bright' (59–61, 63–4). This leads to a damning indictment of nineteenth-century middle-class values:

> Oh, I am tired!
> Tired, tired, of this bland smiling slavery,
> Monotonous waste of life. And while we fools
> Are making curtsies and brave compliments
> To our rare century, and, courtierly,
> Swaddling our strength in trammels of soft silk,
> The rotten depths grow rottener.   (234–40)

In 'An Inventor' (1870) the speaker has dedicated his life to creating an unnamed new machine but has never quite managed to get the 'workings perfected, the life in it; / And there's the flaw again, the petty flaw' (2–3). He is only too aware of how his unrealized financial 'success' has impacted on his family: 'they lack all / Save the bare needs which only paupers lack' (32–3). Within a matter of lines he is capable of delusional hope and then deflated anxiety as to the final outcome of his life's work:

> I know that I shall find my secret yet
> And make my creature here another power
> To change a world's whole life; but that achieved
> Whom will the world thank for it? Me perhaps;
> Perhaps some other, who, with after touch,
> Shall make the springs run easier . . .   (174–9)

'A Painter' (1870) can be compared with Browning's 'Andrea del Sarto', but has a contemporary setting. The poem is also notable for its astonishing single sentence covering lines four to thirty-seven. The painter of the title has completed his masterpiece and is aware of how it falls 'so far short / Of what I aimed at' (2–3). The very long sentence tellingly starts with 'If' (4) and charts the painter's regrets that had circumstances been different, so might have been the art produced. He indulges in a fantasy of imagining his work to have been found worthy by 'Another public than our May-fair crowds, / Raphael and Michael Angelo' (35–6). But the harsh reality is that he is 'a poor man and must earn' (40) and thus 'Must be a hack' (58) and turn out lesser, sentimental paintings that 'will sell' (53). There is pathos in Webster's poem: where del Sarto has a character flaw, the unnamed painter is worn down by social circumstances. He is aware that a 'severer connoisseur' (82) of his work will spot his talent and think 'He ought to take / Two or three years at least of study, draw / More than he paints, scan how the masters did it, / Go to school in Rome' (90–4), and also that he has 'descend[ed] / To dull apprentice plodding' (94–5). As in 'Andrea del Sarto', our painter is married, and the poem is addressed to his wife, but it is laden with much heavier economic hardship: he is acutely conscious of the 'enduring' (186) of his wife and children because he has not become 'a more successful man' (164). Our sympathy rather than judgement is exercised here. Characteristic of almost all Webster's monologues, a point comes where his self-questioning becomes a very questioning of the self:

> For I know there is in me
> Another power than what men's eyes yet find

In these poor works of mine. But who can tell
If now I ever shall become myself?   (124–7)

Webster's speakers can all be encompassed in a phrase used in 'A Preacher' (1870): 'I seem / Divided from myself' (50–1). The question of selfhood is key in Webster's work and we repeatedly see female speakers confronting an 'other' self in a mirror image. Her speakers are full of various kinds of longing, and all engage in self-questioning about their identity: 'I have not yet learned to know myself: / I am so other than I was, so strange' (14–15) says the alleged Happiest Girl in the World.

Webster's work was acclaimed in its own day, although notably critics extolled the 'strength' of her writing. She avoids the pejorative put-downs given to some women's poetry by seeming to have a 'masculine' quality in her work, which 'meant an intellectual, socio-political content' (Leighton, 1992, p. 167). She appears in Alfred Miles's *The Poets and Poetry of the Century* (1891–7), but her dramatic monologues were not included. Times change, because Byron has recently referred to her as 'the key woman writer of monologues' (Byron, 2003, p. 27) and this is hard to dispute. As in Browning, there is a 'conversational immediacy' (Byron, 2003, p. 102) to Webster's monologues: she mimics the rhythms of the speaking voice effectively. In the first edition of *Portraits* (1870) the initial word of run-on lines was not capitalized, making this also a typographically radical volume (although the capitals were re-instated later). Her verse is less 'jagged' than Browning's, however, and any reader wishing to gain an understanding of how to produce metrical blank verse could do far worse than study such a consummate mistress as Webster.

'A Castaway': 'The Silly Rules This Silly World / Makes About Women!'

In February 1858 a letter appeared in *The Times* under the heading 'The Great Social Evil'. This was a response to a previous letter, signed 'One More Unfortunate', which had appeared in January. The second letter describes the impoverished childhood of a pretty girl whose father was a brickmaker, and who, at fifteen 'commenced my career as what you better classes call a prostitute' (Greenblatt, 2006, p. 1593). But now she has money:

> I pay business visits to my tradespeople, the most fashionable of the West-end. My milliners, my silk-mercers, my bootmaker know, all of them, who I am and how I live, and they solicit my patronage as earnestly and cringingly as if I were Madam, the lady of the right rev. patron of the Society for the Suppression of Vice.   (p. 1594)

The writer of this letter asks some very forthright questions: 'what if I am a prostitute, what business has society to abuse me? . . . If I am a hideous cancer in society, are not the causes of the disease to be sought in the rottenness of the carcass?' (p. 1594). The impact of these words is because they come from a prostitute herself. She speaks back to power: all the official discourses which surround (and construct) the Victorian prostitute are written by men.

Webster's finest monologue does the same. As Christine Sutphin notes, 'Prostitutes in Victorian literature rarely have a voice . . . and that is one reason why "A Castaway" . . . is so remarkable'. The poem is also remarkable because '[Webster] did what no other respectable writer had done to the same degree . . . she gave narrative authority, psychological complexity, and a knowledge of social forces to a prostitute persona' (Sutphin, 2000, p. 514). 'A Castaway' opens with the speaker, Eulalie (see line 202), reflecting on the gap between her younger, innocent self, and the 'me / Who am . . . me' (25–6) she is now. This is done via the imagined setting of her re-reading a 'Poor little diary' (1) from her girlhood years. The Eulalie who looks back on her younger preoccupations regards them as proscribed by a very limited sense of what a woman's life could be: 'Did I live so content in such a life, / Seeking no larger scope' (9–10) she asks. Early in this 630-line poem Eulalie raises the audacious question of 'ambition, (was there ever life / That could forego that?)' (15–16). Many Victorian women were indeed forced to forego ambition, or never recognized it as theirs in the first place, so Eulalie's placing of ambition as a preface to her move into what is almost a career as a prostitute is making a point about the circumscriptions placed on middle-class women's lives.

Once again we find a female character in front of a mirror (27). Eulalie is well aware her beauty is 'The dearest thing I have. Why, 'tis my all, / Let me make much of it' (39–40). She also comments, wryly, on her modesty – the word is used six times in fourteen lines (46–58). Like the writer of *The Times* letter, Eulalie is very comfortably off: 'I have a home / All velvet and marquetrie and pastilles . . . And I set fashions and wear cobweb lace' (70–1, 73). One of the pleasures of this monologue is its spirited attempt at defiance in the face of so many narratives that constrain the way the fallen woman should think about herself. As Leighton says, 'the poem is a magnificent, panoramic indictment of many of the cherished values of Victorian England' (Leighton, 1992, p. 196). If Eulalie considers herself modest, she also considers herself engaged in an honourable trade, saying 'I know of worse that are called honourable' (80). She then goes on to list practically all the (male) professions of her day. Although Eulalie will later say 'I hate men' (258) her acerbic comments are not just aimed at them; she has plenty to say about the wives of the 'fine husbands' (102) who are her clients:

> Oh! those shrill carping virtues, safely housed
> From reach of even a smile that should put red
> On a decorous cheek, who rail at us
> With such a spiteful scorn and rancorousness,
> (Which maybe is half envy at the heart) . . .   (113–17)

By contrast, Eulalie is able to say of herself 'I have looked coolly on my what and why, / And I accept myself' (136–37). This is an extraordinary statement within a literary representation of a Victorian fallen woman. However, this comes relatively early on, and a more sustained reading of the poem must acknowledge 'Eulalie's profound ambivalence' (Sutphin, 2000, p. 520). She may well use the religious tract she has been sent as fire tinder (169) but – like many of Webster's other monologists – she warms herself alone, and aloneness is something Eulalie fears: 'Quiet is hell, I say – as if a woman / Could bear to sit alone, quiet all day, / And loathe herself and sicken on her thoughts' (236–8).

In the best dramatic monologues the implied dramatic scenario becomes part of the meaning of the poem, and this is the case here, as Eulalie's initial reading of her youthful diary instigates the train of thought which carries through the entire poem, namely the gap between her past (innocent) self and her present. Eulalie questions personally whether she 'could . . . fit me to my former self?' (216) but later this becomes an astute wider observation on how Victorian society treats women it considers sexually transgressive: 'the prudent world . . . will not have / The woman fallen once lift up herself . . . / Lest she should fall again' (514, 516–18). This ultimate societal condemnation of the fallen woman is not something even Eulalie can fully resist taking into her own self-construction.

We learn that Eulalie did enter one of the Magdalene refuges set up to help women out of prostitution but she 'could not bear it' (240). Had she been found any work it would have been very low-paid: 'More sempstresses than shirts; / And defter hands at white work [embroidery] than are mine' (266–7). The connection between seamstresses and prostitution – the former turning to the latter when they could not get work – had been made in the investigations of journalist Henry Mayhew. Eulalie is also aware of what the 1851 census revealed, that there was a surplus of half a million women over men. What are all these women to do if they cannot take up their right and proper calling of becoming some man's wife? Her caustic suggestion rivals Jonathan Swift's in 'A Modest Proposal' (1729): 'if it were law, / Say, every year, in due percentages . . . To kill off female infants, 'twould make room' (300–1, 303).

'A Castaway' reveals itself as a damning denunciation of the constraints on women's lives generally. As more of Eulalie's back story emerges we learn she was also once a governess. But her memories of such an 'insipid treadmill life' (330) in a 'safe dull place' (347) once again become the spur to a wider criticism of the vapid education meted out to girls. To Eulalie it doesn't even fit them for getting married: 'Who wants a wife to know weeds' Latin names? / Who ever chose a girl for saying dates?' (374–5). It is flippantly said, but the exclamation 'the silly rules this silly world / Makes about women!' (377–8) is surely one of 'A Castaway's' key points, if not also a lynchpin of Webster's female-narrated monologues more generally. For there is no escape from these 'silly rules', however much Webster's women characters might critique them; they restrict and deform her speakers' sense of self.

How are we to respond to Eulalie saying she is 'the thing / Of shame and rottenness, the animal / That feed men's lusts and prey on them' (393–5)? The reader may be reluctant to believe that this is what she thinks of herself, in the light of her spirited taking on of Victorian society. But Eulalie's bravado is a brittle thing, and it is precisely the ambivalence in her characterization that makes this monologue so fine. The latter part of the poem focuses on Eulalie's memories of her brother, Clement, who 'stopped his brotherhood some years ago' (482). More space is given to her sadness over the loss of this relationship than any other, including with the father of her deceased baby. In speaking out at such length about being a 'professional' fallen woman Eulalie seems to evade the male-defined discourses of her day on prostitution such as William Lecky's *The History of European Morals* (1869) which say she is 'that unhappy being whose very name is shame to speak' (Leighton, 1992, p. 197). Imagining the response of her sister-in-law if she realized her husband has a sister who is a prostitute Eulalie mocks 'To think how she would look – Her fright, poor thing!' (619). But in the next lines the emotions shift: 'I could laugh outright . . . or else, / For I feel near it, roll on the ground and sob' (620–1). Is scorn so very far from shame, for 'after all, there's not much difference / Between the two sometimes' (622–3)? No one has obviously overheard Eulalie, challenging the classic notion that there must always be at least an implied, if not 'real' auditor in the Victorian dramatic monologue. So to whom is she speaking? In one sense the implied auditor is the very society that tells her who (and what) she is. It has been clear throughout the poem that she does not like being alone, and the poem ends with a bell ringing and another prostitute friend arriving for a gossip (how different if it was a client!). In the quiet of her loneliness she can much less resist the discourses that construct her as a 'thing / Of shame'.

It is clear that reading 'Jenny' and 'A Castaway' alongside each other makes for interesting comparisons (see Brown, 1991). Virginia Blain turns from 'A Castaway' back to 'Jenny' and notes 'it is interesting what uneasy gaps and cover-ups suddenly appear, and how much more patronizing its (male) narrator becomes' (Blain, 2001, p. 179). If it is the case that women poets often have a closer level of sympathy to their speakers than male writers of the monologue, it is also true that 'their target is more usually the systems that produce the speakers than the speakers themselves' (Byron, 2003, p. 87).

Reading

Brown, Susan (1991), 'Economical Representations: Dante Gabriel Rossetti's "Jenny", Augusta Webster's "A Castaway", and the Campaign Against the Contagious Diseases Acts', *Victorian Review* 17:1, pp. 78–95.

Leighton, Angela (1989), '"Because Men Made the Laws": The Fallen Woman and the Woman Poet', *Victorian Poetry* 27:2, pp. 109–27.

— (1992), *Victorian Women Poets: Writing Against the Heart*. Hemel Hempstead: Harvester Wheatsheaf.

McGann, Jerome (2000), *Dante Gabriel Rossetti and the Game that Must Be Lost*. New Haven: Yale University Press.

The Rossetti Archive: www.rossettiarchive.org

Research

● Compare 'Jenny' and 'A Castaway'. Consider differences in perspective, tone and the speaker as male 'client' versus the speaker as prostitute. Do you read 'Jenny' differently after you've read 'A Castaway'?

● Using the Rossetti Archive or books on Pre-Raphaelite art consider Rossetti's drawings and unfinished painting of *Found*. How do setting these alongside 'Jenny' enhance your understanding of both?

● How is the speaker of any of Webster's monologues aware of the constraints within which they live in Victorian society?

● How effective are any of Webster's monologues, or 'Jenny', as dramatic monologues? How are they different from the monologue style of Browning?

8

Fin de siècle poetries

Amy Levy

Amy Levy's work is significant not only for its exploration of various 'outsider' identities but also because it defines a new urban poetics of the fin de siècle. Born into an Anglo-Jewish family in 1861 Levy lived her short life at a point when increased possibilities were opening up for both Jews and women (English Jews were given full political rights in 1858). Levy's was the first generation of women to go to university and she was one of the very first Jewish women to attend Newnham College, Cambridge, from 1879 to 1881. Levy's Jewish heritage also played an important part in her writing life: she wrote non-fictional articles for the *Jewish Chronicle* and published a novel, *Reuben Sachs* (1888), about Jewish life. The novel was controversial, as it deployed anti-Semitic stereotypes which the Jewish community at large was keen to counter. In order for Levy to establish a poetic identity she also had to take on the implicit equation of English poetry as inherently Christian, as articulated by John Keble and Matthew Arnold (Scheinberg, 2002, p. 205).

Linda Hunt Beckman writes that 'an apprehension of the devaluation of women and the need to widen their opportunities were integral to Levy's sense of self and of society' (Beckman, 2000, p. 6) and Levy is aware of some of the issues associated with the New Woman in the 1890s. The New Woman is undoubtedly a figure of modernity at the fin de siècle, but she is also 'an unrealizable ideal of urban female liberation' (Goody, 2006, p. 468) in that numerous New Woman fictions are ahead of actual women's circumstances in terms of what they imagine for their female characters. Goody writes of Levy's similar interest in 'impossible, irreconcilable figures who nonetheless serve to delineate a space of possibility' (ibid.).

'Xantippe' and 'A Minor Poet'

The title poem of Levy's first volume, *Xantippe and Other Verse* (1881) is a dramatic monologue in the Augusta Webster tradition and articulates the frustrations of the wife of Athenian philosopher Socrates. Xantippe has passed into legend as a bad-tempered, shrewish character, but Levy portrays her as thwarted by the limited expectations of her own culture. As a young woman Xantippe's 'soul . . . yearned for knowledge' (38) and she is well aware that society expects her to learn 'My lesson of dumb patience' (51). Xantippe's memories of her youthful 'vague desires, those hopes and fears, / Those eager longings, strong, though undefined' (30–1) seem very similar to the desires, hopes and fears of Amy Levy's generation of young, intelligent women. The poem hinges on the gendered distinction made between mind/soul and flesh/body and how this impacts on Xantippe and Socrates' married relationship: 'the high philosopher . . . Deigned not to stoop to touch so slight a thing / As the fine fabric of a woman's brain' (119, 121–2). The view of Xantippe as a mere 'angry and awkward wife' is given an origin and rationale in Levy's retelling: Xantippe observes Socrates teaching his disciples and hears his reasoning as to why Aspasia, mistress of Pericles, is allowed entrance into the male circle of philosophers. Socrates regards Aspasia as 'beyond the way / Of women nobly gifted: women's frail – / Her body rarely stands the test of soul' (171–3), and this prompts a spirited outburst by Xantippe at the way her husband limits women's capacities. The poem further exploits gendered stereotypes in the contrast between Xantippe's 'hot passion[ate]' speech (192) and the dismissively rational responses of Plato and Socrates. The latter asks Xantippe 'from what philosophies / Didst cull the sapient notion of thy words?' (213–14), knowing fully well that she cannot debate on their terms. This controlling powerplay strikes Xantippe 'Dumb, crushed with all that weight of cold contempt' (216).

As well as dramatizing debates about gender, knowledge and power, Levy skilfully exploits the drama of the scenes she evokes. As a response to the above Xantippe angrily flings down the wine-skin she is carrying and flees 'across the threshold, hair unbound – / White garment stained to redness' (223–4). She resists the male philosophers' attempts to deny her as woman, as body: the red wine staining her clothing evokes menstrual blood. There is no resolving 'happy ending' to this poem; rather 'Levy's dramatic monologues focus on representing speakers who stand in opposition to certain dominant cultural beliefs, and as a result find no authorizing audience to validate their poetic speech' (Scheinberg, 2002, p. 212). Xantippe realizes there is no place for the woman she aspires to be within the philosophic framework embodied by her husband. Translating this back to the early 1880s the poem strikes a note of anxiety and uncertainty: as Judith Willson says, 'there were few patterns for the lives of single, educated, independent women, or by which others could interpret them' at this time (Willson, 2006, p. 173). But 'Xantippe' is also notable for its great ambition: Levy's poetic career begins with a defiant 'speaking back' to one of the founding fathers of Western philosophy.

Levy's self-proclaimed poetic identity as one who does not write from the centre is consolidated in *A Minor Poet and Other Verse* (1884). As a revised and expanded edition of her first volume this too contains several dramatic monologues, although the lyric voice that will define Levy's last volume is also evident. The volume's epigraph is a poem entitled 'To a Dead Poet', written for James Thomson, who had died in 1882. Thomson is best known for his long, phantasmagoric poem 'The City of Dreadful Night' (1874), and its relentless bleakness is clearly influential on Levy. After Thomson's death Levy wrote a sympathetic article on 'James Thomson: A Minor Poet' (1883) and she understood from personal experience his struggles with depression. Levy writes of Thomson's 'mental suffering' as a form of 'grey pain' (Willson, 2006, p. 177) and the speaker of 'A Minor Poet' has lived with something similar. The dramatic setting of this poem opens with him 'turn[ing] the key / Sharp in the lock. Click!' (1–2) within his 'bare, small room' (76) in order to attempt suicide for the third time. During the poem the speaker is actually successful, drinking in the sunlight 'Across that

endless sea of London roofs' (109) along with a phial of poison, so
the poem partly represents his last thoughts. Levy's minor poet is all
too aware that at the metaphoric feast of life laid out for humankind
'There are not seats for all!' (151) and there are hints of a romantic 'hunger' (155, 158, 162) too: 'There was a woman once . . .
she did not break my heart, / Yet haply had her heart been otherwise / Mine had not now been broken' (173, 75–7). Although Levy's
speaker is male here, it is also widely thought that Levy herself
was lesbian, and numerous of her lyric poems have either female
or ambiguously-gendered addressees. Here the ventriloquizing of a
voice in the dramatic monologue allows her to articulate same-sex
longing, in an era that had no linguistic or cultural framework to
recognize such love between women.

As the speaker of 'A Minor Poet' is alone there is no obvious
implied auditor; however, the minor poet's perspectives are in
implicit dialogue with the other named character in the poem, the
speaker's friend Tom Leigh. After the first suicide attempt Tom
'Burst in, and drew the phial from my hand . . . And lectured me a
lecture . . . freshly culled / From works of newest culture' (8, 10–12).
Tom represents a kind of Arnoldian commentator who offers universal platitudes to console (and admonish) his suicidal friend. Levy's
speaker resists this, and in doing so asserts both his individuality and
his minority status: 'I am myself, as each man is himself – / Feels
his own pain, joys his own joy, and loves / With his own love, no
other's' (21–3). However, because the speaker *does* commit suicide,
and thus effectively exits the poem at line 184, Tom's voice takes
over the substantial Epilogue. Echoing the opening of the poem it is
Tom who 'burst[s] in' (185) again and finds his friend dead. Although
Tom says he has 'no word at all to say' (217) he has already by this
point said quite a lot, and Levy thus dramatizes how 'minor' voices
are all too quickly appropriated by major ones. The question which
ends the poem shows that Tom cannot understand his friend's act
outside of the moralizing that he has imbibed through 'the works of
newest culture' (12) he has read.

The German critic Walter Benjamin, writing on the ultimate modern
poet of the nineteenth century – Baudelaire – said 'It is understand-
able if a person becomes exhausted and takes refuge in death.
Modernity must stand under the sign of suicide, an act which seals a

heroic will that makes no concessions to a mentality inimical toward this will' (Eiland and Jennings, 2003, p. 45). Levy's minor poet, and indeed Levy herself, seem to herald this distinctive response.

Levy's lyrics: 'Ballade of an Omnibus' and 'Ballade of a Special Edition'

The innovative nature of Levy's London-based poetics are increasingly being recognized, particularly in relation to her final posthumous volume *A London Plane-Tree and Other Verse* (1889). The volume is prefaced by a note that says 'The proofs of this volume were corrected by the Author about a week before her death [by suicide]'. Although many poets will make London life their subject in the 1890s Levy pre-dates them. While Levy could deserve a place in what W. B. Yeats would term the 'tragic generation' of fin-de-siècle poets, the mythologizing of the period that followed almost exclusively focussed on men. As a result, critics have failed to recognize Levy's 'most extraordinary and revolutionary idea: that *fin-de-siècle* poetics should celebrate the fluid character of the modern world and become passengers of modernity' (Vadillo, 2005, p. 61).

Ana Parejo Vadillo has noted that – influenced by Baudelaire – the figure of the *flâneur* has been central to later nineteenth-century poetics, but she argues that new forms of urban transport (omnibuses, trams and the Metropolitan Railway [underground]) also influence the perspectives and poetics of a poet such as Levy. In the opening 'London' section of the volume the speaker is almost always on the move, within the urban setting. If she is away from London, as in 'The Village Garden', 'The city calls me with her old persistence, / The city calls me – I arise and go' (15–16). The eleven poems which open *A London Plane-Tree* are a veritable love letter to London. They are full of vitality, and belie the view of Levy as melancholic. As has also been noted, this final volume of poems is a *lyric* volume – and hence the speakers of the poems speak with the lyric 'I'. Goody suggests that 'It is through the space of the city that Levy is enabled to write the specificity of her own unauthorized, ambiguous, "minor" voice' (Goody, 2006, p. 461).

Like other later nineteenth-century poets Levy was interested in experimenting with poetic forms. In particular she uses the French ballade form (also used by D. G. Rossetti and Swinburne) in two of the London poems that deal with contemporary subjects. The ballade's form follows three stanzas of eight lines, rhyming ababbcbc, with the final line of each stanza repeated at the end of each. It then concludes with a four-line 'envoi', rhyming a(b)ca(b)c. 'Ballade of an Omnibus' opens thus:

> Some men to carriages aspire;
> On some the costly hansoms wait;
> Some seek a fly, on job or hire;
> Some mount the trotting steed, elate.
> I envy not the rich and great,
> A wandering minstrel, poor and free,
> I am contented with my fate –
> An omnibus suffices me.   (1–8)

The speaker here eshews more old-fashioned and elitist modes of transport. To experience the city in the most modern way is to be a passenger and this is open to women as well as men. In 1929 Katie Levy Solomon, Amy's sister, sent 'Ballade of an Omnibus' to a London newspaper, along with a letter stating that 'The writer was among the first women . . . to show herself on the top of omnibuses' (Beckman, 2000, p. 139). The poem also charts how new forms of urban travel offer new ways of seeing: 'The scene whereof I cannot tire, / The human tale of love and hate . . . Unfolds itself, rolls by . . .' (19–20, 22) in an almost filmic manner.

'Ballade of a Special Edition' focuses on a new 'London type': the newsboy who hawks the evening edition of the tabloid newspaper, complete with sensational headlines and journalism. The opening image of him as a 'Bird of ill omen, flapping wide / The pinion of a printed sheet' (2–3) is grotesquely effective, and entirely subsumes the natural to the (hu)man-made, in a move characteristic of the anti-Romantic turn of some late-Victorian urban poetry. The repeating refrain of this 'Ballade' cleverly becomes the newsboy's sales pitch cry of 'A double murder in Mile End!' (8, 16, 24, 28). The poem deplores what the newsboy represents, as the public, 'selling' face of a journalism that trades in 'great catastrophe' (23), and the 'envoi' attempts to banish him. For the speaker it is the newsboy who is the 'Fiend' (25) and not anyone whom the newspaper writes about, and ultimately the suggestion is that the double murder in Mile End is 'apocryphal' (27), although Levy's poem also evokes the notorious Whitechapel Murders of 1888.

Arthur Symons

Arthur Symons (1865–1945) was one of the key figures of the fin de siècle as essayist, editor, translator, critic and – not least – poet. He knew everyone worth knowing in later nineteenth-century letters, literature and art and such was his industry as a writer that Oscar Wilde called him 'Symons Ltd.'. As a young man Symons admired Browning and his first book-length work was *An Introduction to the Study of Browning* (1886). The older poet's influence is clear in some of the dramatic monologues and character studies included in Symons' first volume of poetry, *Days and Nights* (1889), but it is not these poems for which he is most remembered. The last poem in the volume – 'The Opium-Smoker' – is a sonnet suggesting more of the experiences for which Symons' poetry is known. The poem holds together two very different tones. In the octet an immersion into the sensation of smoking opium is presented:

> I am engulfed, and drown deliciously.
> Soft music like a perfume, and sweet light
> Golden with audible odours exquisite,
> Swathe me with cerements for eternity.   (1–4)

But the poem's sestet completely changes the mood, as the poem itself embodies the stark difference between the drug-induced state in which 'Time is no more' (5) and the tawdry immediacy of the speaker's surroundings:

> Also I have this garret which I rent,
> This bed of straw, and this that was a chair,
> This worn-out body like a tattered tent,

This crust, of which the rats have eaten part,
This pipe of opium; rage, remorse, despair;
This soul at pawn and this delirious heart.   (9–14)

The repeating use of 'This' underscores the harsh return to reality
after the narcotic wears off. Symons' poetry captures a decadent,
end-of-century mood of excess and ennui, in which pleasures and
sensations are pursued for their own sake, aside from a concern with
morality. But the fleeting nature of the encounters and ecstasies that
litter Symons' poetry only emphasize the ephemeral nature of all
life: decadence, as its very name suggests, is haunted by decay and
death.

Symons is, as a website dedicated to him says, 'The poet of
crumpled bedsheets and of gaslit streets'. He is poetically, aesthetically and spiritually the love-child of Swinburne and Dante Gabriel
Rossetti (or Baudelaire and Verlaine). Symons had his finger on
the fading pulse of the fin de siècle, and published 'The Decadent
Movement in Literature' in 1893. This celebrated essay, which drew
on Symons' knowledge of the French décadents – the Goncourt
brothers, Maurice Maeterlinck, Joris Karl Huysmans and poet Paul
Verlaine – established a language for what Symons termed 'this representative literature of today . . . [which is] a new and beautiful and
interesting disease'. Decadent literature is 'typical of a civilization
grown over-luxurious, over-inquiring, too languid for relief of action,
too uncertain for any emphasis in opinion or in conduct' (Holdsworth,
2003, pp. 72, 73).

Symons had poems and essays published in *The Yellow Book*,
and then became editor of its spiritual successor, *The Savoy* in 1896.
After the 1895 Wilde trials Aubrey Beardsley was sacked as *The
Yellow Book's* art editor which meant Symons could poach him to
be just as risqué for *The Savoy*. Symons wrote one of the first significant accounts of Beardsley's work in 1898 after his death, and
while critics have suggested that Symons' capacity for recreating
various key figures from the 1890s contributed significantly to the
mythologizing of the decade (see Snodgrass, 1990), his later account
of Beardsley as 'the satirist of an age without convictions' seems
apt (1929; Holdsworth, 2003, p. 97). Holdsworth suggests that the
phrase is pertinent to Symons himself, who was acutely aware that

'an increasingly scientific, materialist, urban culture was altering the nature of contemporary experience, [and] that the artist was losing his sense of an audience' (p. 11). What place for the poet with his [sic] over-refined attention to language and form in an era of mass print culture? The emergence of tabloid newspapers such as *The Daily Mail* in 1896 cause Symons to reflect in 'Fact in Literature' (1904) that 'a newspaper is a thing meant to be not only forgotten but destroyed. With the deliberate destruction of print, the respect for printed literature vanished, and a single term came to be used for the poem and the "news item". What had once been an art for the few became a trade for the many . . .' (Holdsworth, 2003, p. 87).

In a memoir Symons writes:

> If ever there was a religion of the eyes, I have devoutly practised that religion. I noted every face that passed me on the pavement; I looked into the omnibuses, the cabs, always with the same eager hope of seeing some beautiful or interesting person, some gracious movement, a delicate expression, which would be gone if I did not catch it as it went.
>
> (*Spiritual Adventures*, 1905; Holdsworth, 2003, p. 89)

As Karen Alkalay-Gut notes, 'Since this type of writer no longer possesses a clearly defined hierarchy of values, everything before him . . . holds equal worth. Consequently, the amount of data to be processed and set in order can prove exhausting' (Alkalay-Gut, 2000, p. 247). Just as this suggests decadent ennui so Symons's modernity as a flâneur of 'the tumultuous night of London' ('April Midnight', 1892, 3) is also clear.

London Nights (1895)

Symons most decadent volume is *London Nights* (1895). Dedicated to Verlaine, the volume attracted something of the same controversy as Swinburne's *Poems and Ballads* nearly thirty years earlier. But as *London Nights* was published by Leonard Smithers, the most notorious of decadent publishers, there was never any likelihood the volume would be withdrawn. The controversy – as with

Swinburne – concerned subject matter. Symons wrote of 'The feverish room and that white bed, / The tumbled skirts upon a chair' ('White Heliotrope', 1–2) and the volume features numerous fleeting sexual encounters, including with prostitutes: 'As I lay on the stranger's bed, / And clasped the stranger-woman I had hired . . .' (To One in Alienation, II', 1–2). He mimics a Baudelairean attitude to women when he writes 'I know the woman has no soul, I know / The woman has no possibilities / Of soul or mind or heart, but merely is / The masterpiece of flesh' ('Idealism' 1–4), and diagnoses the contemporary condition of his society when he says 'The modern malady of love is nerves. / . . . Nerves, nerves! O folly of a child who dreams / Of heaven, and, waking in the darkness, screams' ('Nerves', 1, 13–14).

But Symons' subject matter also marks out his modernity. He celebrates the artifice and anti-natural qualities of cosmopolitan city life: cigarettes, gaslight, 'Maquillage' (1892) and a flagrant writing of 'the chance romances of the streets' ('Stella Maris', 4) are all new subjects for poetry. In his essay 'Modernity in Verse' (1892) Symons praises the poetry of W. E. Henley who had published *The Song of the Sword* (renamed *London Voluntaries*) in the same year. Henley's modernity is because of his

> sense of the poetry of cities . . . Here . . . is a poet who can so enlarge the limits of his verse as to take in London. And I think that might be the test of poetry which professes to be modern: its capacity for dealing with London, with what one sees there, indoors and out.
>
> To be modern in poetry, to represent . . . the world as it is to-day, to be modern and yet poetical is, perhaps, the most difficult . . . of all artistic achievements.   (Symons, 1924, pp. 45–6)

Henley's 'In Hospital' sequence – in rhymed and unrhymed verse – charts the experience of sustained hospital treatment and surgery. 'Here is verse which seems . . . to be made out of our nerves', writes Symons, 'verse which . . . . almost physically hurts us' (Symons, 1924, p. 50). This attention to the extremes of contemporary living, and a sense that nothing about modern life should be left out of poetry, clearly influenced Symons' own practice.

Music-hall modernity: 'Prologue', 'Nora on the Pavement', 'La Mélinite: Moulin Rouge'

Modernity was providing new subjects for poetry, and if popular culture threatened the survival of poetry, it also provided new topics for it. This is seen in Symons' repeating focus on the music hall and stage dancers. He was fascinated by music-hall culture, and in 1892 became a reviewer for the *Star* newspaper of performances at the Alhambra and Empire theatres. In 1889 the Moulin Rouge dancing cabaret opened in Montmartre, Paris, and Symons frequented it. He had liaisons and various infatuations with dancers on both the London and Paris stage which are refracted into numerous poems. In the 'Prologue' (note the theatrical term) to *London Nights* the speaker is the punter/voyeur in the audience, but also the dancer becomes a mirror-image of the self:

> My life is like a music-hall,
> Where, in the impotence of rage,
> Chained by enchantment to my stall,
> I see myself upon the stage
> Dance to amuse a music-hall. (1–5)

In the third stanza a kind of self-contempt is manifest in the way he talks of himself-as-dancer:

> My very self that turns and trips,
> Painted, pathetically gay,
> An empty song upon the lips
> In make-believe of holiday:
> I, I, this thing that turns and trips! (11–15)

By association, this is the implicit view the speaker holds of the female dancer, and the artificiality of the 'riotous' (19) setting, and the almost literal waste of time that the speaker regards attending the music-hall as, are part of the fascination-repulsion tension which animates Symons' poetry. Karl Beckson regards this poem as 'a metaphor for the poet in the process of composing the self-enclosed

poem' (Beckson, 1987, p. 118) and it is important to note the use
of quintains (five-line stanzas) in this and other poems about dance
such as 'Nora on the Pavement' and 'La Mélinite: Moulin Rouge'.
The attention to form in poetry at the fin de siècle – in particular care-
fully patterned repeating rhyme schemes – is influenced by French
forms such as the villanelle and rondeau. Both D. G. Rossetti and
Henley, among others, had written poems using quintains. The use
of repeating lines or words to rhyme creates a self-circling sense in
the poem, as a way of representing the solipsism and self-enclosure
of the dancer.

In his essay 'The World as Ballet' (1898) Symons sets out his own
'philosophy' of dance. The dancer is associated with a primitive freedom from restraint. She is disinhibited, but also (on stage) offered up
to the viewer for his [sic] enjoyment: '[dancers] seem to sum up in
themselves the appeal of everything in the world that is passing, and
coloured, and to be enjoyed' (Holdsworth, 2003, p. 81). The dancer
responds bodily to music, and Symons is aware of Walter Pater's
influential aesthetic dictum in *The Renaissance* (1873) that 'all art
constantly aspires towards the condition of music':

> Nothing is stated, there is no intrusion of words used for the
> irrelevant purpose of describing; a world rises before one,
> the picture lasts only long enough to have been there: and the
> dancer . . . evokes, from her mere beautiful motion, idea, sensation,
> all that one need ever know of event.   (Holdsworth, 2003, p. 82)

In 'Nora on the Pavement' Nora is freed from the confines of the
stage (with echoes, perhaps, of Ibsen's Nora in *A Doll's House*
[1879], which Symons saw in the first London production in 1889).
She dances 'Petulant and bewildered' (6, 10) on the 'midnight pavement' (5). For Symons Nora becomes a 'living symbol' ('The World
as Ballet', Holdsworth, 2003, p. 82), an emblem of the utterly disinhibited self which is 'Leaping and joyous, keeping time alone / With
Life's capricious rhythm' (17–18):

> It is the very Nora;
> Child, and most blithe, and wild as any elf,
> And innocently spendthrift of herself,

And guileless and most unbeguiled,
Herself at last, leaps free the very Nora.   (25–9)

The woman/child/innocence/simple/natural equations are not hard
to see here and it is possible to regard this as yet another example
of Symons' essentializing attitude to 'Woman', contrasting with the
over-refined sophistication of the decadent male. But Beckson also
notes that Symons' use of dance functions 'as a means of understanding and expressing his vision of art and the ambiguities of illusion and
reality' (Beckson, 1987, p. 77). 'Bird-like' (28) Nora is what the male
poet can no longer be – similar to Baudelaire's albatross of 30 years
earlier he is grounded, ungainly, and a subject of ridicule.

La Mélinite was the stage name of the French dancer Jane Avril,
who famously appeared on Toulouse-Lautrec's fin-de-siècle posters.
In 'La Mélinite: Moulin Rouge' the use of doubled rhyming words is
taken to its extreme, with internal repeating words added as well:

Alone, apart, one dancer watches
Her mirrored, morbid grace;
Before the mirror, face to face,
Alone she watches
Her morbid, vague, ambiguous grace.   (11–15)

Here the dancer needs the mirror – no one else – to know how to
dance. She 'dances for her own delight' (28), although the poem's
speaker also sees all. Various aesthetic intertexts are also present,
as line thirteen echoes James McNeill Whistler's painting *Symphony
in White, No. 2 (The Little White Girl)* (1864), which had Swinburne's
poem 'Before the Mirror' (1866) originally appended to its frame.
The dancer as *femme fatale*, as narcissistically self-absorbed, is also
there in Wilde's notorious *Salomé* (1894), and W. B. Yeats, Symons'
friend and co-member of The Rhymers' Club, would famously ask at
the end of 'Among School Children' 'How can we know the dancer
from the dance?' (1926).

Symons' enduring reputation rests on his 'help[ing] shape fin de
siècle literature and early Modernism in England' (Beckson, 1987,
p. 53). Yeats, Pound and Eliot all cited his influence, and his more
imagistic poems, such as 'Colour Studies: At Dieppe', point the

way to a visual poetry shorn of unwelcome Victorian didacticism. Reviewing *London Nights*, the *Pall Mall Gazette* called him a 'very dirty-minded man' (1895), which Symons no doubt took as something of a compliment. The fleeting, the ephemeral, the uncertain, the *carpe diem* spirit tainted by a weary melancholy – all inflect and infect his memorably modern musical lyrics.

Reading

Alkalay-Gut, Karen (2000), 'Aesthetic and Decadent Poetry', in *The Cambridge Companion to Victorian Poetry*, ed. Joseph Bristow, pp. 228–54. Cambridge: Cambridge University Press.

Beckman, Linda Hunt (2000), *Amy Levy: Her Life and Letters*. Athens, OH: Ohio University Press.

Beckson, Karl (1987), *Arthur Symons: A Life*. Oxford: Oxford University Press.

Hetherington, Naomi and Nadia Valman, eds (2010), *Amy Levy: Critical Essays*. Athens, OH: Ohio University Press.

Thain, Marion (2007), 'Poetry', in *The Cambridge Companion to the Fin de Siècle*, ed. Gail Marshall, pp. 223–40. Cambridge: Cambridge University Press.

Research

- Levy's poems can be read as voiced by, or seen through the consciousness of ex-centric outsiders. Discuss one of her poems in the light of this suggestion.

- How do Levy's poems portray her engagement with late nineteenth-century modernity?

- In what ways does Levy's poetry explore some of the same issues as 'New Woman' fiction of the 1880s–90s?

- Discuss a Symons poem that captures the decadent spirit of the fin de siècle.

- In 'Prologue', 'Nora on the Pavement' and 'La Mélinite' how is Symons using the *form* of the poems and features such as repetition to embody his view of the dancer/the dance?

PART THREE

Wider contexts

9

Critical contexts

The amount of Victorian poetry criticism is extensive. This chapter highlights just some of the critical trends in the field over the past thirty or so years. Mostly the focus is not on works about single poets, although 'the concept of the author as a valuable and distinct individual is still very much alive' in many considerations of Victorian poetry (Richards, 2001 [1986], p. xi).

Victorian poetry criticism 1950s–80s

Criticism from the 1950–1970s tends to focus on a limited range of male poets. Robert Langbaum's influential study of the dramatic monologue, *The Poetry of Experience* (1957), concentrates on Robert Browning and Tennyson for its discussion of Victorian poets, and bases the key insight of how readers split sympathy and judgement in responding to speakers of dramatic monologues predominantly on Browning. In *The Alien Vision of Victorian Poetry* E. D. H. Johnson highlights a 'double awareness' in the best Victorian writing, which is due to 'modern society ha[ving] originated tendencies inimical to the life of the creative imagination' (Johnson, 1952, pp. ix, xi). Tennyson, Browning and Arnold demonstrate this. Isobel Armstrong's *The Major Victorian Poets: Reconsiderations* (1969) considers the same 'big three', as theirs was the Victorian poetry that T. S. Eliot and influential critics I. A. Richards and F. R. Leavis reacted against earlier in the twentieth century. Room is also made for Clough and Hopkins. J. Hillis Miller's *The Disappearance of God* (1963) discusses de Quincey, Robert Browning, Emily Brontë, Arnold and Hopkins, and makes explicit the centrality of poetry to discussions of Victorian doubt and faith. This is consolidated in R. L. Brett's anthology *Poems of Faith and Doubt* (1965).

It is important to mention works that have made available extracts of Victorian poetics, for to understand Victorian poetry more completely it is necessary to engage with what the Victorians themselves said about it. The 'Critical Heritage' series – mostly published in the 1970s–80s and organized by a writer's name – offered contemporary reviews of works at the time of publication, and subsequent selected critical responses. Armstrong's *Victorian Scrutinies: Reviews of Poetry 1830–1870* (1972), Joseph Bristow's *The Victorian Poet: Poetics and Persona* (1986) and Donald Thomas's *The Post-Romantics* (1990) are all relevant, with Bristow offering a particularly good introduction. There is no specific book that focuses solely on later Victorian poetics by way of such extracts.

The relationship between Victorian poetry and philosophy is explored in Isobel Armstrong's *Language as Living Form in Nineteenth Century Poetry* (1982) and W. D. Shaw's *The Lucid Veil: Poetic Truth in the Victorian Age* (1986). Both are challenging but rewarding reads. Armstrong reads Hopkins, Wordsworth, Blake, Shelley, Tennyson and Browning in dialogue with Hegel and Marx, arguing that 'the language and form of nineteenth-century poetry [is] a model of the structure of consciousness or being itself' (Armstrong, 1982, p. xiii). Armstrong's focus on the continuity of Romantic and Victorian poets is a feature of her work generally, while Shaw's work situates Victorian poetics in their philosophical contexts in the same way M. H. Abrams' *The Mirror and the Lamp* did for Romanticism.

Bernard Richards' *English Poetry of the Victorian Period, 1830–1890* (1986) announced itself as the first general history of Victorian poetry since the 1930s, and an accompanying anthology edited by Richards appeared at the same time. Such works are influential in defining a broad field of study for a generation of students. Morris, Swinburne, Christina and D. G. Rossetti, Elizabeth Barrett Browning, Meredith and Dorset dialect poet William Barnes are all discussed. While strictly outside the book's 1890 limit, Hardy and Hopkins are also included. Regarding Victorian poetry as transitional between

Romanticism and Modernism, Richards argues that 'one witnesses a variety of strategies adopted by the poets faced with the challenging and alarming modern world, ranging from acceptance and acquiescence . . . to hostility, protest, and evasion' (Richards, 1986, p. 7). The framework is thematic, encouraging a contextualization of differing poems alongside each other, and also in relation to themes such as 'The Past', 'Nature and Science', 'Victorian Satire' and 'Religion'.

Expanding the canon: Diversified voices

If Richards' book helped define the wide scope of Victorian poetry, and expanded the sense of which poets needed to make up that discussion in the 1980s, the 1990s make clear who has still been left out. Many women poets were forgotten for much of the twentieth century, when a more masculinist modernist poetics meant a wholesale turning away from the seemingly embarrassing 'gush of the feminine' (Armstrong, 1995, p. 13). Recent re-evaluations, however, have asked us to think again when we approach a 'women['s] . . . poetic culture that welcomed and celebrated intense passions' (Armstrong and Bristow, 1996, p. xxviii).

Angela Leighton's *Victorian Women Poets: Writing Against the Heart* (1992) paved the way, offering consideration of Felicia Hemans and 'L.E.L.' as well as Augusta Webster, Michael Field, Alice Meynell and Charlotte Mew alongside the more familiar Barrett Browning and Christina Rossetti. There is increased recognition that in order for Victorian women poets to get a fair hearing it is necessary to consider them separately from male poets. Three collections of essays on Victorian women poets appear in close succession: Joseph Bristow (ed.), *Victorian Women Poets* (1995), Tess Cosslett (ed.), *Victorian Women Poets* (1996), and Angela Leighton (ed.), *Victorian Women Poets: A Critical Reader* (1996). Leighton's is the only collection to go substantially beyond the female triumvirate of Brontë, Barrett Browning and Rossetti, with essays also on Adelaide Procter, Mary Coleridge, Michael Field and Rosamund Marriott Watson. In the more general sections of these readers, significant essays which have helped define the field appear. Dorothy Mermin's 'The Damsel, the Knight, and the Victorian Woman Poet' (1986) articulated the problematic double-bind that the Victorian woman poet faced as she tried to situate herself in the already (ef)feminized sphere of poetry which represented a retreat from the world for male poets, but which for her was 'a move toward public engagement and self-assertion in the masculine world' (Mermin, 1986, p. 68). Mermin's '"The fruitful feud of hers and his": Sameness, Difference, and Gender in Victorian Poetry' (1995) also explores the gendered complexities for both male and female poets. Her final suggestion is that 'in some important sense all the Victorian poets, male and female, can be read as women' (Mermin, 1995, p. 165).

By the middle of the 1990s two important anthologies of women's poetry had been published, and several anthologies are included in this critical chapter because editorial projects can be significant critical interventions, particularly if they make available poets and poems hitherto largely ignored. Angela Leighton and Margaret Reynolds' *Victorian Women Poets: An Anthology* (1995) contains selections from fifty poets and Isobel Armstrong and Joseph Bristow's *Nineteenth-Century Women Poets* (1996) features more than one hundred. Armstrong's desire to make explicit the connections and continuities between the 'Romantic' and 'Victorian' is seen in her choice of title and also in a subsequent volume of essays edited with Virginia Blain, *Women's Poetry: Late Romantic to Late Victorian, 1830–1900* (1999). Both anthologies contain important introductions. *Nineteenth-Century Women Poets* notes that as a result of the rediscovery of these women poets, 'new relations emerge, both between newly read poems and the largely male canon, and between women poets themselves' (Armstrong and Bristow, 1996, p. xxiii). A collection of extracts outlining women's contributions to Victorian poetics remains to be done.

In 1985 Eve Sedgwick's *Between Men: English Literature and Male Homosocial Desire* came out. As a foundational work of queer theory the book had other designs than Victorian poetry alone, but the inclusion of a chapter on *The Princess* was significant as much for the inclusion of Tennyson as Sedgwick's reading of the work. The suggestion that as central and canonical a Victorian poet as Tennyson was implicated in readings which explicitly focussed on male same-sex desire was also taken up by Alan Sinfield in his important book *Alfred Tennyson* (1986). A great deal of work has since been produced which is attentive to masculinity, (ef)feminacy and sexuality in Victorian poetry, such as James Najaran's *Victorian Keats: Manliness, Sexuality and Desire* (2002), which traces the influence of Keats's sensuous language and potential androgyny on a number of male Victorian poets. In relation to women's poetry Virginia Blain has questioned why we 'should narrow our readerly options by turning our backs too soon on the lesbian in any text' (Blain, 1999, p. 142) and she encourages readers to 'remain open' to the still-provocative presence of same-sex sexuality and actively queer reading in approaches to Victorian poetry.

The second edition of Richards' *English Poetry of the Victorian Period* in 2001 included a new chapter on women poets (and one on nonsense poetry) but by the new millennium this approach seems outmoded. Joseph Bristow, ed. *The Cambridge Companion to Victorian Poetry* (2000), and Richard Cronin, Alison Chapman and Antony Harrison, eds. *A Companion to Victorian Poetry* (2002) approach the complexity, nuance and diversity of Victorian poetry by way of multi-authored volumes. This allows many more critical voices to be heard, and although gender is approached as a distinct category for discussion via chapters on 'The Victorian poetess' and 'The poetry of Victorian masculinities' (in *The Cambridge Companion*) there is much more recognition of the ways women's and men's poetry together creates the field. Kathy Psomiades offers a useful overview of changing critical attitudes to Victorian poetry via discussion of 'The Lady of Shalott' in *The Cambridge Companion*, and Cynthia Scheinberg considers Victorian religious poetry by focusing on Jewish as well as Christian contexts. The *Companion to Victorian Poetry* is divided into three parts, the first of which focuses on 'Varieties and Forms'. As well as the more usual chapters (e.g. on Dramatic Monologue, Elegy, The Pre-Raphaelite School) there are also considerations of 'Hymn', 'Verse Drama', 'Poetry in Translation', 'Tractarian Poetry' and 'The Spasmodics'.

The second section of the *Companion*, 'Production, Distribution and Reception', highlights another area of development in Victorian studies, which is an interest in Victorian publishing practices and a heightened attention to the physical and material make up of specific books themselves and the relationship of text, image and book-as-artefact. As numerous works of Victorian poetry are either illustrated, or are conceived as aesthetically coherent books, this is a rich strand of criticism. Behind such work hovers the influence of Jerome McGann's *The Textual Condition* (1991), and McGann's outworking of the necessity of considering all aspects of a text's embodied materiality and publishing contexts, ranging from manuscripts to book design, is the online *Rossetti Archive* (1993–2008). Dante Gabriel Rossetti's position as poet and painter makes him exemplary (McGann, 2000), but McGann and others have also stressed material making in the poetry of William Morris (McGann, 1993; Miles, 1999; Helsinger, 2008). Poets regarded as Pre-Raphaelite are central to this approach, and Lorraine Janzen Kooistra's work on Christina Rossetti is also exemplary (Kooistra, 2002).

Politics versus aesthetics

Isobel Armstrong's *Victorian Poetry: Poetry, Poetics and Politics* (1993) is an ambitious and impressive rereading of Victorian poetry. Armstrong argues that the Victorian poets engaged with a situation which set the realm of art (and hence poetry) apart from practical experience for the first time. Increasing mechanization was producing the Marxist division of self which produces alienated labour, and Victorian poetry comes into being under these conditions. At the same time Armstrong remains highly attentive that 'to read a Victorian poem is to be made acutely aware . . . it is made of language' (Armstrong, 1993, p. 11). She focuses on the concept of the 'double poem' as the characteristic form of Victorian poetry, produced through dramatic monologues, frame narratives, dream poems or dialogues. The monologue form ultimately gives rise to a scepticism about any utterance of the lyric 'I', however confessional a poem might seem. Armstrong considers a wider range of women and men poets than any previous single-authored similar work. As the book is broadly organized by poet the bunching of all women poets into one chapter still has its controversies, although this long (and influential) chapter is at its centre.

The need to reassert the politics of Victorian poetry highlights one of the central tensions that beset almost any discussion of Victorian poems. Victorian studies now is often broadly materialist and places high regard on the situating of literary texts within their wider cultural contexts. As many key works are in significant dialogue with the complex issues of their day there can be a temptation to mine the poem for 'what it says about' any given topic. However, all poetry is shaped language which organizes itself in formal, aesthetic ways, and indeed, in the terms of the New Critical school of criticism of the 1950s onwards, it would be perfectly possible to consider a Victorian (or any) poem entirely on its own terms, largely sealed off from any consideration of context. Matthew Reynolds takes issue with Armstrong's use of politics, suggesting that 'to emphasize that sexual relations, epistemology, and language are . . . themselves intrinsically "political" is to play down the question of how they connect with what people in the nineteenth century generally meant by politics' (Reynolds, 2001, p. 9). Although interested in the relationship of longer Victorian poems to 'actual' political contexts of the period, Reynolds is also sceptical of the 'poetry-as-journalism approach [which] assumes that, whatever a poem's genre is, its defining context is always provided by its immediate historical surroundings' (pp. 15–16). This scepticism is right, and Armstrong's concept of the doubleness of Victorian poems maintains an openness to necessary ambiguity in any interpretive engagement. Herbert Tucker's *Epic: Britain's Heroic Muse, 1790–1910* (2008) frames the long nineteenth-century as the context for a discussion of many now-forgotten long poems (as well as some better known) which had ambitions to fuse myth into nationalism as a way of telling the Victorian spirit of the age. He refutes our constructions of literary history that have made epic an 'irrelevance' (Tucker, 2008, p. 4).

Until relatively recently Victorian poetry has been a field which favours the voices of the privileged over the marginal. If women poets are now also sitting at the table the next bastion to break down concerns class. Martha Vicinus's *The Industrial Muse* (1974) started this important work off and her conclusion then, that 'what we call literature . . . is what the middle class – and not the working class – produced. Our definition of literature and our canons of taste are class bound', is still true to a fair extent today, including in relation to Victorian poetry (Vicinus, 1974, p. 1). Vicinus focuses on street ballads and broadsides, Chartist poetry, dialect poetry and the self-educated poet. Brian Maidment's *The Poorhouse*

Fugitives: Self-Taught Poets and Poetry in Victorian Britian (1987) still remains the only anthology focused on male working-class poets, although Valentine Cunningham's comprehensive anthology *The Victorians: An Anthology of Poetry and Poetics* (2000) does include some working-class poetry. Mike Sanders' *The Poetry of Chartism* (2009) homes in on the poetics and poetry of the period's first radical political movement. The related focus on women poets has again lagged behind, with the work of Florence Boos central. Her anthology on *Working-Class Women Poets in Victorian Britain* came out in 2008 (see also Boos, 2000, 2001, 2002).

Fin-de-siècle poetry criticism

Fin-de-siècle poetry has often featured as one aspect of wider discussions about the 1890s, and as mentioned in Chapter 8 poets such as Symons and Yeats were in no small part responsible for the mythologizing of the decade that resulted in the personality-driven memoir of the early twentieth century. Graham Hough's *The Last Romantics* (1949), taking its title from a line in Yeats's 'Coole Park and Ballylee' (1931), traces Yeats's influences back through the Rhymers' Club, Pater, Morris, D. G. Rossetti and Ruskin. Derek Stanford's *Poets of the 'Nineties* (1965) continues the earlier trend by announcing itself as a 'Biographical Anthology'. R. K. R. Thornton's *Poetry of the 1890s* (1970) follows, but importantly is organized thematically, highlighting aestheticism, the presence of London, Catholic religiosity, the flavours and hues of fin-de-siècle love poetry, its obsession with death, and the influence of France. More significantly, once the full-blown 'rediscovery' of the fin de siècle is well underway during the 1990s, Marion Thain joins Thornton to re-edit the volume and produces the first real acknowledgement that numerous women poets were also writing in the later nineteenth century (1997, 2nd edn). Linda Hughes's anthology on *New Woman Poets* followed in 2001. As the Victorian fin de siècle has always been more inclusive of various dissident or 'othered' voices than the high Victorian period, much new work on late Victorian poetry seems more at ease with the inclusion of women poets. Joseph Bristow, ed. *The Fin-de-Siècle Poem: English Literary Culture in the 1890s* (2005) is a good example of this integrated approach. Lisa Rodensky's anthology of decadent poetry (2006) recognizes that decadence did not only belong to the boys, and features Rosamund Marriot Watson, Michael Field and Anglo-Indian poet Sarojini Naidu. As Thain and Ana Parejo Vadillo comment when introducing a special issue of *Victorian Poetry* on fin-de-siècle women poets, 'the work of women poets can now be studied under a set of headings gleaned from a sense of the period as a whole, rather than under those specific to a gender-defined remit' (Thain and Vadillo, 2006, p. 392). Vadillo's book on *Women Poets and Urban Aestheticism* (2005), whilst focused in detail on Meynell, Watson, Levy and Field, is also a contribution to late-Victorian poetics as a whole. Her argument that the travelling passenger (and not just the walking flâneur) of London's late-nineteenth-century streets 'is constitutive of a new urban epistemology' is suggestive (Vadillo, 2005, p. 25).

Nicholas Frankel's elegant *Masking the Text: Essays on Literature and Mediation in the 1890s* (2009) takes poetry as a predominant focus and uses the fin-de-siècle motif of 'the mask' as a means of paying attention to the material specifics of a range of poetic works, from Wilde's *A House of Pomegranates* to the *Books of the Rhymers Club* to Morris's Kelmscott Press publications. As Frankel notes, 'no literary or artistic work comes independent of its medium . . . artistic media are in fact constitutive of meaning' (Frankel, 2009, p. 24).

Victorian poetry criticism now

In 2004 a special issue of the journal *Victorian Poetry* surveyed the current state of Victorian Poetry Studies, focusing in particular on a new generation of scholars. The volume opens with a witty overview by Armstrong, entitled 'The Victorian Poetry Party' (Armstrong, 2004). Armstrong notes various trends within the essays and reasserts a commitment to the same methodological doubleness she finds in contributors who 'believe that the bringing together of history and form, culture and language, politics and the aesthetic, is the key, the never-ending struggle, of writing about any poetry' (p. 21). Not for the first time she also states that 'it begins to look more and more limiting to use the epithet "Victorian"' when considering poetry of the (long) nineteenth century' (p. 24). She ends by affirming that 'we should be unapologetic about claiming aesthetic power for poetry' (p. 25) and offers several lively suggestions for teaching 'The Lady of Shalott'.

The tension between 'the dominance of various kinds of theory-based interpretive discourse and the privileging of social and cultural contextualizations' and readings which focus on more 'intrinsic' or 'aesthetic' qualities in Victorian poetry is also the concern of Kerry McSweeney's *What's the Import: Nineteenth-Century Poems and Contemporary Critical Practice* (2007, p. 1). For McSweeney the former have flourished at the expense of the latter and he thus offers an 'aesthetic model' (p. 7) in approaching several English and American poets.

I conclude with two recent works on Victorian poetry. Linda Hughes's *Cambridge Introduction to Victorian Poetry* (2010) reminds readers that 'Victorian poetry was inseparable from the mass print culture within which it found an audience' (p. xi), and pays attention to the appearance of poems in periodicals (where many were often first published) and newspapers. For example, Thomas Hood's 'The Song of the Shirt' first appeared in a Christmas issue of *Punch* in December 1843, and 'the surrounding Christmas contents and the season itself, with its emphasis on benevolence and compassion, intensified the impact of the poem' (p. 93). Similarly Tennyson's 'The Charge of the Light Brigade', itself a response to an article in *The Times* which gave the poem its (in)famous line 'Someone had blundered', appeared in weekly newspaper *The Examiner* in 1854. Its periodical publication aided popularity and facilitated Tennyson's ability to respond immediately to a contemporary situation (p. 93). Hughes also reminds us that much discussion and debate *about* poetry also went on in periodicals, via both reviews and essays. Her book also includes a section on the appearance of Victorian poems in novels of the period.

Finally, where are we now? Valentine Cunningham's *Victorian Poetry Now: Poets, Poems, Poetics* (2011) offers many suggestions. As editor of *The Victorians: An Anthology of Poetry and Poetics* (2000), containing selections by 158 poets, Cunningham has good reason to be aware of 'just how many poets there were and how much they wrote' (p. 3). The Victorian double poem, which is 'intrinsically aesthetic yet opens a space for cultural politics' (Hughes, 2011, p. 7), is most effectively responded to in a criticism that aims to do the same:

> my mission is to show how poets, and so their poems, come marinaded in politics and economics, the wars of contemporary ideas, and how they are utterly conscious of their times. And poets, and so their poems [are] . . . in the main, highly self-conscious poetically, aesthetically.   (Cunningham, 2011, p. vii)

On the back of *Victorian Poetry Now* John Sutherland writes 'Whole-field study is rare in literary scholarship because it demands so much of the single scholar' and as the field of Victorian poetry becomes ever larger few may attempt the 'magnum opus' book. But Cunningham is well placed to do so, and his readable and wide-ranging work contains valuable and substantial sections focusing on language, sound, rhyme and repetition, as well as a smörgåsbord account of the diversity and range of the poetry of the period. He defiantly asserts at the outset that he is 'not afraid of the fact that poems are produced by poets, actual men and women, living in the real world, who are the actual thinking, feeling, writing channels for all the contents and discontents which poems evince' (p. vii). Cunningham also challenges the modernist dismissal of Victorian poetry (in effect, a dismissal of Victorian *poetics*) and he emphasizes the links and influences between Victorian and Modernist poetry. Thus the place to end this chapter and to lead us into the final one is the suggestion that 'If the supposed border between the Victorian and Modernist exists at all, it's a tumbledown, porous affair' (p. 467).

Reading and research

- Reading for this chapter is any of the references above.
- Read the Introductions to Leighton and Reynolds' *Victorian Women Poets: An Anthology* (1995) and Armstrong and Bristow's *Nineteenth-Century Women Poets* (1996). What issues do they raise about women's poetry in the nineteenth

century? Is it still necessary to consider women's poetry separately from men's poetry?

● Will there always be some Victorian poets regarded as more-or-less canonical/central?

● From your reading of some of the works mentioned in this chapter (e.g. Bristow's *Cambridge Companion to Victorian Poetry* [2000] and Cronin et al.'s *A Companion to Victorian Poetry* [2002]) what factors influence changing approaches to Victorian poetry?

● What do you make of the 'politics versus aesthetics' debate (or content versus form) in relation to reading Victorian poetry?

● How should the field of Victorian poetry studies continue to develop? Should more poets keep being added to anthology mixes?

10

Afterlives and adaptations

It is appropriate that this book should have a chapter entitled 'Afterlives' as two of the poets who cross the divide between Victorian poetry and what followed engage profoundly with the questions of faith and doubt that concerned many of their predecessors. This final chapter thus opens with discussions of Gerard Manley Hopkins and Thomas Hardy, before considering Modernist responses to Victorian poetry. It also charts some of the very diverse ways in which Victorian poets and poems have lived on into the twentieth and twenty-first centuries.

Gerard Manley Hopkins: Victorian modernist

Although many of Hopkins's well-known poems were written in the 1870s–80s, a full edition of his poems was not published until 1918, and recognition of his extraordinary innovativeness only happened in the 1930s. He has been described as 'the greatest modern English religious poet' (Storey, 1992, p. xi). Hopkins's poetry is suffused with his Catholic faith and an immanent sense of God in all things, especially nature. If this latter point connects him to the Romantics, his use of language pushes towards being post-Victorian.

Hopkins attended Balliol College, Oxford, where his most important friend was Robert Bridges. Bridges published Hopkins's poetry after his death and was one of his main readers during his lifetime.

Frequently Bridges did not understand his friend's poems, meaning Hopkins had to explain them to him. Thus 'his letters to Bridges contain one of the most revealing defences we possess of any poet's practice and poetic beliefs' (Storey, 1992, p. 89). Balliol had a significant poetic pedigree (Arnold and Clough attended), and the Oxford of the period was also still engaged with doctrinal debates concerning the direction of the Church of England. The Tractarian movement of the 1830s–40s had ultimately led to its leader, John Henry Newman, 'defecting' to Catholicism in 1845. Hopkins too decided to leave the Anglican Church and was accepted into the Catholic faith by Newman at Birmingham Oratory, in 1866. He became a Jesuit priest in 1877.

After seven years poetic silence, and having destroyed most of his early poetry in an act of spiritual renunciation, Hopkins wrote 'The Wreck of the Deutschland' in 1875. It is his greatest longer poem and contains 'already fully-fledged and with complete assurance, all his technical innovations' (Storey, 1992, p. 67). The poem was inspired by the tragedy of the German ship S S Deutschland, which sank off the English coast en route to New York. Among those drowned were five Franciscan nuns fleeing Germany's anti-Catholic Falk Laws. It is in two parts: the first enacts a spiritual struggle between the speaker and Christ/God, reminiscent of John Donne's 'Holy Sonnets'; the second focuses on the shipwreck and martyrdom of the nuns:

> I did say yes
> O at lightning and lashed rod;
> Thou heardest me truer than tongue confess
> Thy terror, O Christ, O God;
> Thou knowest the walls, altar and hour and night:
> The swoon of a heart that the sweep and the hurl of thee trod
> Hard down with a horror of height:
> And the midriff astrain with leaning of, laced with fire of stress.
> (9–16)

The experience of being 'master[ed]' (1) by God is evoked with the same violence as the Deutschland in the storm. It's important to *hear* Hopkins's poetry and characteristic of his work is a dense sound pattern of mutating and echoing consonant and vowel sounds. Hence 'yes' and 'confess' echo with 'heard*est*' and 'Chr*ist*'; 'say' is almost reversed in 'yes'; 'knowest' echoes 'heardest'; 'altar', 'hour', 'heart', 'hurl' are all connected, as are 'truer', 'terror' and trod'; 'swoon' mutates into 'sweep'; 'knowest', 'swoon', 'down' and 'horror'; are all assonant half rhymes; midriff is picked up by 'fire'; astrain' is echoed by 'stress'.

In his journals and letters Hopkins set out his own poetics. He is associated with 'Sprung Rhythm', adapting the use of metrical feet in Victorian poetry. The commonest – iambic (x /), trochaic (/ x), anapæstic (x x /), dactylic (/ x x) – all involve one stressed beat followed or preceded by one or two off-beats. Typically the whole poem will utilize the same underlying metre. In Sprung Rhythm a foot – which is usually two or three syllables – can be anything from one to four syllables, and the stressed beat falls on the first beat. Hence there are four different possibilities of Sprung Rhythm feet: (/) (/ x) (/ x x) (/ x x x). A poetic line can mix these up as it wishes. Sprung Rhythm is moving towards free verse, but still constrains poetic lines within a metrics that allows for greater flexibility than that available within classical Victorian metres. In particular, using a single stressed syllable as an acceptable foot means that stressed syllables can appear next to each other, whereas usually they are separated by at least one off-beat.

Hopkins also coined the terms 'inscape' and 'instress'. Inscape refers to 'the beauty of pattern which expresses a thing's inner or essential form' (Storey, 1992, p. 60). 'Instress', incorporating the notion of poetic 'stress', is the energy of inscape, both intrinsic to the object itself, but also in terms of the energy or force it exerts on the perceiver. In 'The Wreck of the Deutschland', Christ's 'mystery must be instressed, stressed' (39).

Hopkins's mature poetry embodies this: he piles verbs into his poems to create a wordscape of immense vitality. Everything in nature points to the presence of God within, the instress to its inscape:

As kingfishers catch fire, dragonflies draw flame;
. . .
Each mortal thing does one thing and the same:
    Deals out that being indoors each one dwells;
    Selves – goes its self; *myself* it speaks and spells,
Crying *What I do is me: for that I came.*   (1, 5–8)

Hopkins also wrote six 'terrible sonnets', which evoke desolation, despair and a sense of abandonment by God. He knew that 'the mind, mind has mountains; cliffs of fall / Frightful, sheer, no-man-fathomed' ('No worst', 9–10). Another of these sonnets opens 'To seem the stranger lies my lot' (1) and although this refers to Hopkins living in Ireland when he wanted to be in England there is also interest in Hopkins's oddity or queerness. His attraction to male beauty and the inherent complexity of his style contribute to the possibility of reading Hopkins queerly. Writing to Bridges in 1879 Hopkins said 'what I am in the habit of calling "inscape" is what I above all aim at in poetry. Now it is the virtue of design, pattern, or inscape to be distinctive and it is the vice of all distinctiveness to become queer' (Hopkins, 2002, p. 235). Julia Saville has suggested that 'sprung rhythm is a key element in . . . Hopkins's poetics of homoerotic asceticism' (Saville, 2000, p. 1).

Hopkins was way ahead of his time in the 1870s–80s. His limited attempts to publish in his own lifetime fell on stony ground, as readers could not understand the poetic terms on which he was working. We now have the privilege of being able to appreciate how astonishing his poetry is. His poems are 'heaven-roysterers, in gay-gangs / they throng; they glitter in marches' ('That Nature is a Heraclitean Fire', 2).

Thomas Hardy: Modern Victorian

Hardy met Tennyson and Robert Browning *and* discussed his work with Virginia Woolf. His career as a poet was a second career, taken up after a conscious decision to stop writing the novels that established his literary reputation. *Jude the Obscure* (1895) was Hardy's last novel. Although Hardy did not start publishing poetry until 1898 his poetic roots go back to the 1860s. Realizing he couldn't make a living out of poetry Hardy trained as an architect, and one of his most descriptive statements (made in 1899) about how he understood his practice as a poet uses an architectural analogy:

> . . . in architecture cunning irregularity is of enormous worth, and . . . he carried on into his verse . . . the Gothic art-principle

in which he had been trained . . . resulting in the 'unforseen' . . . character of his metres and stanzas, that of stress rather than of syllable, poetic texture rather than poetic veneer . . . He shaped his poetry accordingly, introducing metrical pauses, and reversed beats.   (Hardy, 1994, pp. 78–9)

This love of the irregularity inherent in Gothic architecture makes Hardy's poetry 'entirely Victorian and consummately modern' (Collins, 1990, p. 14). His messing up of the smooth musicality of strict rhythm marks him as the end of the Romantic line, as his poems bear content that bespeaks his late-Victorian modernity. Hardy is a profoundly elegiac poet, but he is the start of the elegy made modern, via poems that do not offer 'transcendence or redemption of loss but immersion in it' (Ramazani, 1994, p. 4).

Some of Hardy's most famous poems were written well into the twentieth century – such as the 1912–13 poems about the death of his first wife Emma. My focus here is on poems published in *Wessex Poems* (1898) or *Poems of the Past and Present* (1901). If Emma's death is one of Hardy's great loss-infused themes, then the death of God is his other. He is 'typical of those late Victorians for whom the "death of God" left a palpable absence' (Armstrong, 2009, p. 13). Hardy is relentlessly post-Darwinian, in that he finds no sign of God in nature. In 'A Sign-Seeker' (1898) the speaker has seen nature's wonders: 'I have seen the lightning-blade, the leaping star, / The cauldrons of the sea in storm' (9–10). But they mean nothing in the face of death:

Such scope is granted not to lives like mine . . .
   I have lain in dead men's beds, have walked
   The tombs of those with whom I had talked,
Called many a gone and goodly one to shape a sign,

And panted for response. But none replies . . .   (41–5)

The echo of *In Memoriam's* rhyme scheme (abba) suggests a negative reply to the attempted optimism of that poem's end. Fifty years later Hardy's universe is silent.

One of the most famous of Hardy's first-published poems is 'Thoughts of Phena', written in response to the death of his cousin,

Tryphena Sparks, in 1890. Hardy is rumoured to have been in love
with her in the 1860s:

> Not a line of her writing have I,
>   Not a thread of her hair,
> No mark of her late time as dame in her dwelling, whereby
>   I may picture her there;
>   And in vain do I urge my unsight
>   To conceive my lost prize
> At her close, whom I knew when her dreams were upbrimming
>   with light,
>   And with laughter her eyes.   (1–8)

Hardy was a highly inventive poet. In more than 900 poems he created over 600 stanza forms. As Dennis Taylor says, 'While [Hardy]
always maintained accentual-syllabic stanza forms, he moved
towards poems composed in unique and complex stanzas increasingly conscious of their own visibility in the manner of the free verse
poem' (Taylor, 1999, p. 201). Here the underlying metre is a lively
anapæstic beat (x x /). While the metre should mean that the 'I' at
the start of line four is an off-beat, the reader stumbles strongly on
to all syllables of 'whereby / I . . .', emphasizing the speaker's loss.
Here also is one of Hardy's oxymoronic coinages of a word with a
negating prefix, in 'unsight'. This also appears in 'Tess's Lament'
(1901) in the line 'I'd have my life unbe' (44), and in 'In Tenebris,
I' (1901), where 'One who, past doubtings all, / Waits in unhope'
(23–4).

Hardy's poetic standing on the cusp between the Victorian and the
Modern is seen in 'The Darkling Thrush', published in *The Graphic* on
29 December 1900. 'Darkling' is a wonderful word with associations
stretching back to Keats's 'Ode to a Nightingale' (1819) via the 'darkling plain' (35) of Arnold's 'Dover Beach'. The speaker 'lean[s] upon
a coppice gate / When frost was spectre-gray' (1–2) amidst the dead
of winter:

> The land's sharp features seemed to be
>   The Century's corpse outleant,
> His crypt the cloudy canopy,
>   The wind his death-lament.   (9–12)

Into this bleak imagining of the century's death erupts 'a full-hearted evensong / Of joy illimited' (19–20). However, the bird that sings as night descends is no youthful herald of a new dawn: he is 'An aged thrush, frail, gaunt, and small' (21) who 'fling[s] his soul / Upon the growing gloom' (23–4). The speaker sees so little cause for 'such ecstatic sound' (26) that he can only think the bird knows of 'Some blessed Hope' (31) of which 'I was unaware' (32). Bearing in mind Hardy's depictions of a post-Darwinian nature as utterly unfeeling, the imputation of 'Hope' to the thrush seems ironic. The bird does not consciously bring hope, but it *does still sing*. There is 'withering honesty and refusal of easy consolation' in Hardy's poetry (Riquelme, 1999, p. 214). Along with his roughed up metrics, these are the keynotes of his modernity.

Hardy is often regarded as the starting point of a modern lyrical strand in English poetry which passes on through Robert Frost, Edward Thomas and Robert Graves. But it is Philip Larkin who most clearly picks up Hardy's mantle in the twentieth century. Larkin's first volume imitated Yeats, often favouring an archetypal vocabulary; but after avidly reading Hardy Larkin's subsequent volumes all sound like – Philip Larkin. Hardy gave Larkin the confidence to find his own distinctive, mid-twentieth-century voice, which is wry, cynical, sometimes disappointed, often sad, and on occasions searingly honest in its refusal to look away from that which is uncomfortable. Like Hardy, Larkin is also still compelled by the 'imaginative and moral beauty' of Christianity (Whalen, 1986, p. 59) in poems such as 'Church Going' and 'Religion'. Larkin is similarly Hardy's disciple in his commitment to a formal, metrical poetry where 'natural rhythms and word-order of speech [are played off] against the artificialities of rhyme and metre' (Larkin, 1983, p. 71). Hardy has not appealed to all poets – R. S. Thomas wrote 'Hardy, for many a major / Poet, is for me just an old stager, / Shuffling about a bogus heath, / Cob-webbed with his Victorian breath' ('Taste', 1970, 21–4). However pamphlet publisher Happen*Stance* recently produced *Who's in the Next Room* (2010), which juxtaposes Hardy's poems with responses from contemporary poets.

Modernist reactions

Eliot, Pound and Yeats regarded modernism as a decisive break with the previous century. Victorian poetry was too much the container for *ideas*, and thus full of an 'empty rhetoric' (Christ, 1984, p. 142). In 1921 Eliot praised Metaphysical poetry over that of subsequent centuries and damned Tennyson and Browning by saying they 'ruminated' (Eliot, 1951, p. 288). He was convinced of *In Memoriam's* greatness, but regarded Tennyson as dwindling into 'the surface flatterer of his own time' (p. 338). Pound's early pronouncements on poetry react against what he regarded as the weaknesses of the Victorians: 'I think we shall look back upon it as a rather blurry, messy . . . sentimentalistic, mannerish sort of a period' (Pound, 1954 [1918], p. 11). Yeats, an original member of the 1890s Rhymers' Club, subsequently wrote 'Swinburne . . . Browning . . . and Tennyson . . . filled their work with what I called "impurities", curiosities about politics, about science, about history, about religion; . . . we must create once more the pure work' (Yeats, 1926, p. 207). Yeats also opens the *Oxford Book of Modern Verse, 1892–1935* (1936) by turning an extract from Walter Pater's discussion of da Vinci's *Mona Lisa* in *The Renaissance* (1873) into a poem. In the short-lived Vorticist journal *Blast* (1914–15) Wyndham Lewis set out in iconoclastic typography numerous things to 'Blast' and 'Bless'. Among those to be 'blasted' are 'CHAOS OF ENOCH ARDENS / laughing Jennys / Ladies with Pains / good-for-nothing Guineveres' (*Blast* 1, 1914).

Such modernist manifestos, with their desire to 'make it new', have been influential on twentieth-century poetics. There is generational rebellion here, as sons shuck off their literary forefathers (Bloom, 1973), but there are also clear influences and connections between Victorian and modernist poetry and poetics. The Browningesque dramatic monologue, separating poet and speaker, is a key influence on Eliot's desire for a more objective poetry as in 'The Love Song of J. Alfred Prufrock' (1915). Eliot also cited Symons' *The Symbolist Movement in Literature* (1899) as having 'affected the course of my life' (Beckson, 1987, p. 200) because it introduced him to Verlaine, Rimbaud and Jules Laforgue – the latter one of the first to experiment with *vers libre* (free verse). Henley's 'In Hospital' sequence and the pervasiveness of the city in later nineteenth-century poetry also point towards Eliot. Browning's influence can also be seen in Pound's *Personae* (1908–10), and *Hugh Selwyn Mauberley* (1920) references Rossetti and Swinburne and quotes the epigraph to 'Jenny'. Early versions of *The Waste Land* also referenced 'Jenny'. Carol Christ suggests that Eliot, Pound and Yeats produced their own 'creative caricature' of the Victorians and argues for continuities between poetry and poetics from the Romantics to the Modernists, with the Victorians as central to that development (Christ, 1984, p. 155). More recently Valentine Cunningham has taken on the 'travestying cliché . . . that Victorian poetry fails to measure up in word-choice and word-arrangement' (Cunningham, 2011, p. 12) as a result of modernist accounts of it.

Are modernist women writers less likely to denounce their forbears? Virginia Woolf's account of 'Killing the Angel in the House' is probably now far better known than Coventry Patmore's poem ('Professions for Women' [1931], Woolf, 2008, p. 142). However, the phrase concerns the need to banish Victorian understandings of gender that restrict women's possibilities rather than being a dismissal of Victorian poetry per se. Woolf takes on the whole enterprise of literary biography via *Flush: A Biography* (1933), offering a quirky account of Elizabeth Barrett Browning as seen through the eyes of her beloved spaniel. Well aware by 1932 that the myth of Elizabeth and Robert had eclipsed Barrett Browning's reputation as a poet, Woolf also wrote a sympathetic essay on *Aurora Leigh* (Woolf, 1965a). She also wrote on Christina Rossetti, whom she regarded as having risen to 'the first place among English women poets' (Woolf, 1965b, p. 202). H[ilda]. D[oolittle]., associated with the Imagism of Pound, wrote a very striking tribute poem 'To William Morris (1834–1896)':

Enemy of earth's desolation,
Husbandman, guardian of peace,
Raise your gonfalon over us,
    Georgius Sanctus . . .   (1950, 1–4; Zilboorg, 2003, p. 305)

The continuing popularity of Victorian poets and poems

However much modernist poets reacted against it, 'Victorian poetry ha[s] entered the popular consciousness' (Cunningham, 2011, p. 14). In a 1995 British poll to find the nation's favourite poem Rudyard

Kipling's 'If' (wr. 1895; pub. 1910) came top, gaining twice as many votes as the runner up, Tennyson's 'The Lady of Shalott' (Jones, 1996). Popular poems such as 'If' and William Henley's 'Invictus' (1875) evoke a certain optimistic stoicism in the face of adversity, and have been co-opted as an aspect of 'British spirit'. If this sounds both masculine and imperialist that is because both were written during the height of the British empire, and 'If' was written as a response to British raids in South Africa.

Certain Victorian poets and poems have become cultural icons and continue to be dialogued with, remade, pastiched and incorporated into other artworks. Often Victorian poems are used in symbolic ways, where the new use or adaptation sets up a dialogue between present and past. Christine Krueger suggests that 'we appeal to Victorian culture in order to think about problems and needs that are not wholly unprecedented' (Krueger, 2000, p. xii) and new engagements with Victorian poems implicitly or explicitly comment on the originals, but also ask us to consider how our present is both like and unlike nineteenth-century contexts.

Laureate legacies: Tennyson, elegy and queer memory

Tennyson's death on 6 October 1892 marked the end of an era. He was afforded all the pomp of a state funeral and poets poured out their elegies to the poet who had made the elegy the period's most popular poetic form (Matthews, 2004). One hundred years later Mick Imlah wrote a sequence of poems entitled 'In Memoriam Alfred Tennyson' which opens with 'No one remembers you at all', but this couldn't be further from the reality. Tennyson is one of the Victorian period's most subsequently cited poets. James Joyce mocks the former Poet Laureate as 'Lawn Tennyson, gentleman poet' in *Ulysses* (1922) (Joyce, 2000, p. 259), and a comic portrait of 'the dirtiest laureate that ever lived' (Truss, 2004, p. 12) features in Lynne Truss's novel *Tennyson's Gift* (1996), set on the Isle of Wight in 1864. A younger Tennyson appears in Adam Foulds's *The Quickening Maze* (2009) although the novel's central focus is John Clare (see Morton, 2009).

Paul Muldoon wrote an anniversary poem in 1992 entitled 'A Tennyson Triptych, 1974' conjuring up the ghostly experience available online of hearing a wax-cylinder recording of Tennyson intoning 'The Charge of the Light Brigade'. While it is perhaps more difficult for us today to take seriously the catastrophe-turned-in-to-heroism sentiments of this poem its *rhythms* remain irresistible to a poet such as Matt Harvey, who turns them into a meditation on not quite managing to get to work on time in 'The Charge of the Late Brigade' (Harvey, 2010, pp. 90–1). The same poem is also inspiration for The Divine Comedy's song *Charge* (on the album *Casanova*, 1996), which uses its tango beat to reimagine the original's war-charge as a hurtle into a sexual encounter. It also features in the 2009 bio-drama film *The Blind Side*, about Michael Oher, who came from an impoverished homeless background to become an American Football star. Oher is given personal tuition to improve his essay grades so he might qualify for a university sports scholarship. To get Oher to engage with Tennyson's poem Sean Tuohy, husband of Leigh Anne Tuohy (who has adopted Michael), convinces Oher that its subject is akin to the Louisiana State University Tigers playing football.

One of Tennyson's major legacies is via *In Memoriam*. Lines from it have passed into popular consciousness ('nature, red in tooth and claw', 'Tis better to have loved and lost / Than never to have loved at all' [a 1985 Eurythmics song has much the same title as the latter]), and it also remains influential as a model for elegiac sequences (e.g. Douglas Dunn's *Elegies* [1985], Christopher Reid's *A Scattering* [2009]). But it is the poem's homoeroticism, and the fact that its Victorian setting renders this both covertly overt and also volubly unspoken, that has motivated contemporary writers. Andrew O'Hagan's *Be Near Me* (2006) takes its title from section 50 of *In Memoriam*. The novel concerns David, a Catholic priest who comes to work in a small Ayrshire parish in Scotland, and who befriends two local youths, Mark and Lisa, with tragic personal consequences. *In Memoriam* is also quoted in the title of Alan Hollinghurst's *The Stranger's Child* (2011), which charts generational change and the (de)formation of literary reputation via the figure of a young, upper-class, Georgian poet, Cecil Valance, who is killed during the First World War. While staying at the home of his Cambridge friend, George Sawle, with whom he is having an affair, Cecil writes a poem titled after the house, 'Two Acres', in the autograph book of George's sister Daphne, with whom he also has a dalliance. After the Great War lines from 'Two Acres' seep into the national consciousness as markers of a lost pastoral Englishness, and subsequent sections of the novel are concerned with the difficulty of bringing into the open the possible homosexual roots of the poem, both to Cecil's own family and also to a wider public. Hari Kunzru has written that *In Memoriam* is 'the paradigmatic high Victorian elegy to male friendship' and how Tennyson 'hovers . . . over [Hollinghurst's] novel as a sort of tutelary spirit' (Kunzru, 2011).

Jaspar Rees queried in 2012 whether 'classic' novel adaptation has reached saturation point and wondered whether 'poetry [has] been considered', mischievously suggesting 'a luscious if low-budget BBC Four account of Tennyson's *In Memoriam*' (Rees, 2012). Until then *In Memoriam* fans will have to make do with such references as O'Hagan's and Hollinghurst's, and more improbable ones such as Princess Nuala reciting the 'Be near me' section watched over by Abe Sapien in the action movie *Hellboy 2: The Golden Army* (2008).

U. A. Fanthorpe deliberately echoes the title of the final part of *Idylls of the King* in 'The Passing of Alfred' (1982). The poem's epigraph records Queen Victoria's account of Tennyson's death: 'He . . . died with his hand on his Shakespeare, and the moon shining full into the window over him . . . A worthy end' (Fanthorpe, 2010, p. 81). The poem appears to contrast the decorous, orderly nature of death 'then' with death 'now', but also recognizes that 'They also died appallingly' (26). Fanthorpe's humorous 'Maud Speaking' (2000) has the eponymous heroine answering back to the poet who created her: 'When I came to the gate alone / You were making eyes at a lily . . .' (1–2). An upbeat recent appropriation of Tennyson is the choice of the last line of 'Ulysses' (1842) – 'To strive, to seek, to find, and not to yield' (70) – as a motivational inscription on the Athletes' Wall at the 2012 London Olympics and Paralympics. However, some interpretations of this poem point out its internal ironies and suggest its message is not purely one of uncomplicated aspiration. Only four lines prior to the end Ulysses says 'We are not now that strength which in old days / Moved earth and heaven' (65–6). These lines from 'Ulysses' also appear in the James Bond movie *Skyfall* (2012).

The still-withdrawing roar of 'Dover Beach'

Another Victorian poem which washes through our cultural memory is Arnold's 'Dover Beach'. It is a quintessential Victorian poem of Englishness and a memorable response to the loss of religious certainty. Anthony Hecht's 'The Dover Bitch' (1967) irreverently engages with the woman in the original, who features as the narrator's addressee in the famous fourth section. Hecht's poem opens colloquially: 'So there stood Matthew Arnold and this girl / With the cliffs of England crumbling away behind them' (1–2). In Hecht's version the narrator 'knew this girl' (6) and every now and then 'We have a drink / And I give her a good time' (25–6). In the permissive 1960s she's not quite as 'true' as Arnold's exhortation urged her to be. The narrator also offers a louche sympathy that to 'be addressed / As a sort of mournful cosmic last resort / Is really tough on a girl' (17–19).

In Ray Bradbury's novel *Fahrenheit 451* (1953) the hero Guy Montag is a fireman in a dystopian future society that has outlawed books. Firemen are employed not to put out fires but to start them if any trace of books is found. In this satire on post-war American consumerism and the emergence of a media-controlled society rebel Montag at one point reads 'Dover Beach' to his vacuous wife and her friends, reducing one of them to tears. Here it is significant that it is *poetry* Montag chooses to read and Arnold is particularly appropriate because of his late-nineteenth-century role as 'guardian of culture'.

Daljit Nagra's 'Look We Have Coming to Dover!' (2007) has as its epigraph line 32 from 'Dover Beach': 'So various, so beautiful, so new'. Nagra offers a poetry that charts the British Indian experience via a vibrant 'Punglish' – a mixture of Punjabi and English. Where 'Dover Beach' looked out anxiously across the English channel 'Look We Have Coming to Dover!' imagines the immigrant experience. The final stanza echoes the last section of 'Dover Beach', but now evokes the fantasy promise of what coming to Britain means:

Imagine my love and I,
our sundry others, Blair'd in the cash
of our beeswax'd cars, our crash clothes, free,

we raise our charged glasses over unparasol'd tables
East, babbling our lingoes, flecked by the chalk of Britannia!
(21–5; Nagra, 2007, p. 32)

'Dover Beach' also features memorably in Ian McEwan's post-9/11 novel *Saturday* (2005), set on Saturday, 15 February 2003, the day of the anti-Iraq-war march in London. A violent and unpredictable man named Baxter, who has been in a minor car collision earlier in the day with the novel's central character, Henry Perowne, neurosurgeon, breaks into Perowne's home and holds his family hostage. Perowne's daughter Daisy is a precocious young poet who has recently published her first collection. As Daisy is forced to strip naked Baxter asks her to recite something from it. Unable to do so her grandfather encourages her to 'Do one you used to say for me' (McEwan, 2006, p. 220) and Daisy thus recites 'Dover Beach', communicated to the reader via Perowne's own misrecognition of Arnold's poem as one of Daisy's own. Baxter also thinks Daisy wrote it and is transfixed: '"It's beautiful. You know that don't you. It's beautiful. And you wrote it."' (p. 222). McEwan makes 'Dover Beach' shimmer with significance at this moment of extreme tension in the twenty-first century, which threatens violence both personally within the Perowne family but also politically via the threat of the Iraq war.

The poem has also provided the name of the 'Sea of Faith Network', founded after the 1984 BBC series hosted by philosopher-theologian Don Cupitt, which aims to 'explor[e] and promot[e] faith as a human creation' (www.sofn.org.uk). Into our multi-cultural, sceptical, and sometimes love-lorn present, where questions of faith versus secularism, and belief versus agnosticism and atheism are still with us, 'Dover Beach' retains its capacity to make us 'Listen!' (9).

'The Lady of Shalott' lives on

Continuing dialogues with 'The Lady of Shalott' have explored central Victorian issues that continue to haunt the twentieth and twenty-first centuries, concerning women, gender (in)equality, sexuality and identity.

American poet Lucy Larcom (1824–93) uses 'Weaving' (1868), which clearly references Tennyson's poem, to make a powerful anti-slavery comment. Larcom's woman weaver is no romanticized vision but an *actual* woman weaver, and Larcom herself was sent to work in the cotton mills in Lowell, Massachusetts, aged eleven. The weaver makes the connection between her own position in the North of America and 'women sad and poor; / Women who walk in garments soiled' (43–4) enslaved on cotton plantations in the South.

Two of the most intriguing twentieth-century responses to the original are Elizabeth Bishop's 'The Gentleman of Shalott' (1936) and Veronica Forrest-Thomson's 'The Lady of Shalott' (1974). Bishop's Gentleman appears to be only half there, with half of him 'a mirrored reflection / somewhere along the line / of what we call the spine' (13–15). The Lady of Shalott's uncertain sense of self is figured as a kind of lack in Tennyson, whereas the Gentleman's precarious identity – 'If the glass slips / he's in a fix – / only one leg, etc.' (33–5) – is something he 'finds exhilarating' (41). Forrest-Thomson's work explores the possibilities and limitations of language and representation. She is interested that the Lady of Shalott is not just 'a creature of fiction; she is an organising formal principle' (Forrest-Thomson, 1978, p. 123) in that 'Shalott' must rhyme with 'Camelot'. The 'meaningless' line 'Bear tear flair dare' (6) parodies the emphasis on repeating rhymes in the original.

Aline Kilmer's 'For All Ladies of Shalott' (1921) utilizes phrases and lines from Tennyson's poem and offers a markedly feminist slant. Once the mirror has cracked and the curse has come 'She only laughed and tried to sing. / But singing, in her song she died. / *She did not profit anything*' (10–12). Into the twenty-first century, UK performance poet Rachel Pantechnicon's 'Lady of Shalott Day' (2003) is not feminist, but *is* funny:

> . . . today is Lady of Shalott Day –
> only once a year, when you have to go into work
> in all your Lady of Shalott gear,
> and if you forget and wear your cardigan and your pop-socks,
> you have to put some money in the Lady of Shalott box.   (7–11)

The poem has also been used in several novels. Agatha Christie's *The Mirror Crack'd from Side to Side* (1962) is a Miss Marple mystery.

Jessica Anderson used the title *Tirra Lirra by the River* (1978) for a novel about her heroine, Nora Porteous, going on a journey of self-discovery. David Benedictus's comic Cambridge-set novel, *Floating Down to Camelot* (1985) features Professor Hilda Leeks giving an entire lecture on the poem (complete with the passing thoughts of her audience) and has a death-obsessed plot. Professor Leeks comments that Tennyson's 'romantic medievalism' (Benedictus, 1985, p. 31) has never gone out of fashion, also seen in Canadian singer-songwriter Loreena McKennitt's setting of the poem (on the album *The Visit*, 1991), and Lincolnshire-based WAG Screen's 2009 filmed dramatization.

'The Lady of Shalott': The visual legacy

WAG Screen's film demonstrates how the legacy of 'The Lady of Shalott' is as much bound up with *visual* responses to the poem as verbal ones. The ubiquity of visual responses to Tennyson's poetry in his own time, and the position of 'The Lady of Shalott' as the most illustrated Victorian text, has carried over into its cultural afterlife. From the famous drawings and paintings of Rossetti, Siddall, Holman-Hunt and Waterhouse, to the first illustrated edition of the poem in 1852 (by 'A Lady') and subsequent editions such as Howard Pyle's experiment in colour printing in 1881, 'The Lady of Shalott' was an integral part of the Victorian visual imagination. In 1894 George Somes Layard published *Tennyson and his Pre-Raphaelite Illustrators: A Book about a Book*, focusing on the Moxon Tennyson (1857), and interest in Tennyson and illustration continues to this day (see Cheshire, 2009). As Lizbeth Goodman reminds us, 'any artist's rendering is at once an interpretation in itself and an influence on viewers who subsequently read or re-read the literary text which inspired it' (Goodman, 1996, p. 29). WAG Screen's film is influenced by John William Waterhouse's most famous painting of *The Lady of Shalott* (1888, Tate Britain). The implicit sexuality of Waterhouse's young woman – with her loose red hair and left hand placed suggestively in her lap – are taken up in contemporary black and white by Charles Keeping in his 1986 illustrated edition where the Lady is repeatedly depicted in see-through clothing.

One frequent visual depiction of 'The Lady of Shalott' is the poem's climactically dramatic moment when Lancelot flashes into the mirror and 'The mirror crack'd from side to side' (115). Florence Rutland's pen and ink *The Lady of Shalott* appeared in *The Yellow Book* (1896) and depicts this crisis. Birmingham School painter Sidney Meteyard's *'I Am Half Sick of Shadows,' Said The Lady of Shalott* (1913) dramatizes the sexual repression implicit in this line, portraying a more mature Lady (hair neatly tied back) who swoons as she weaves an image of Lancelot into her tapestry. Modern fantasy artist Linda Garland pictures the (adolescent) Lady looking out cautiously through the cracked mirror/window (1992), but the most interesting and challenging late-twentieth-century visual response is Shelagh Horvitz's, whose 1981 pencil drawing, *'I Am Half Sick of Shadows . . .'*, presents the viewer with an emaciated, even anorexic, naked woman who turns her back on her (small) tapestry and sits hunched up staring into space. The bare torso of a man appears in the reflecting mirror as well as the outlines of two other ghostly faces. This image is far more uncomfortable than others that are aesthetically beautiful and objectify the Lady as available to a male gaze as she hovers on the brink of adult female sexuality. It is no coincidence that from the very outset of depictions of the Lady of Shalott one of the other favoured moments to 'fix' visually is the Lady floating down to Camelot – passive, prone and if not yet quite dead, soon to be so.

If this very Victorian equation of 'female sexuality equals death' is a long way from what we might hope the twenty-first century is saying to and about young women it is nonetheless the case that the myth of 'The Lady of Shalott' lives on. Californian singer-songwriter and electric violinist Emilie Autumn features her 'Victoriandustrial' version of *Shalott* on her 2006 album *The Opheliac*. In Autumn's harpsichord-inflected gothic rock the Lady of Shalott is death-driven but still very much alive.

'Goblin Market' and the after-gaze

The other poem whose illustrated status in the Victorian period has influenced its afterlife is Christina Rossetti's 'Goblin Market'.

Numerous illustrated editions of the poem have followed on from those of D. G. Rossetti (1862) and Laurence Housman (1893) (see Kooistra, 1994, 1999, 2002). 'Goblin Market' also offers ample possibilities for the visual representation of young women on the brink of adult sexuality, with all its pleasures and dangers. Arthur Rackham illustrated the poem in 1933 and provided an influential image to accompany the line 'White and golden Lizzie stood' (408) when she is being assailed by the goblins but is resisting their attempts to tread and jostle her. Rackham's edition was aimed at the children's market, but adult magazine *Playboy* notoriously reprinted the entire poem as 'A Ribald Classic' in 1973 with its own version of Rackham's illustration. Lizzie is depicted in similar pose to her 1933 counterpart, although now semi-naked, and the goblins are energetically thrusting on to her a mixture of erect phalluses and 'fruits' that evoke any number of sexual parts. Kinuko Craft, the Japanese-American illustrator, also produced a detailed Lady of Shalott image for the cover of Patricia McKillip's fantasy novel *The House at Stony Wood* (2000). The Rackham image is again used in John Bolton's adult comic version of *Goblin Market* in 1984, where the potential of the line 'For there is no friend like a sister' for an adult male market is also exploited. Martin Ware's illustrations for a 1980 edition, which depict a goblin who is half-rat, half-naked man, seem to play more on adolescent girls' fears. Powering us from the present back to the poem's first publication the online Rossetti Archive features a stained glass square made by Morris and Co. (c. 1862) with a rather more friendly and asexual bunch of animal goblins depicted. From its very outset the meaning of this poem has been connected to visual representations, and this has profoundly influenced the poem's afterlife.

Elizabeth and Robert

Elizabeth Barrett Browning's reputation as a poet was overwhelmed in the first part of the twentieth century by the compelling myth of Elizabeth and Robert, poetry-writing lovers. Rudolf Besier's play *The Barretts of Wimpole Street* (1930) aided this, and subsequently spawned films, a musical and a 1982 television series. The animated Peanuts cartoon *Be My Valentine, Charlie Brown* (1975) has the character Sally receiving a valentine candy heart on which appears Barrett Browning's most famous sonnet, 'How do I love thee?', in its entirety. Jo Shapcott juxtaposes Robert and Elizabeth with another renowned writing couple, Robert Lowell and Elizabeth Hardwick, in a sequence of poems in *Electroplating the Baby* (1988). Shapcott uses these poems – including 'Fun with Robert and Elizabeth', 'The Goose and the Gander' and 'Robert Watches Elizabeth Knitting' – to explore 'the dialogue between masculine and feminine writing' (Gregson, 2011, p. 20). Laura Fish's novel *Strange Music* (2008) reworks both the poetry and the life via an 'imaginative re-vision of Barrett Browning's "The Runaway Slave at Pilgrim Point"' (Heilmann and Llewellyn, 2010, p. 82), drawing on Barratt Browning's corre-spondence and information about her father's Jamaican estates.

Robert Browning features in Michael Dibdin's murder mystery *A Rich Full Death* (1986), set in nineteenth-century Florence, and Gabrielle Kim's *His Last Duchess* (2010) provides a backstory for the infamously absent subject of Browning's most famous monologue. Richard Howard's 'Nikolaus Mardruz to his Master Ferdinand, Count of Tyrol, 1565' (1999) is a *tour de force* sequel to 'My Last Duchess', in which the envoy sent to the Duke of Ferrara now reports back to his own master, in a monologue as cunningly convoluted and schem-ing as the original. Howard is a particularly skilled monologist, having won the Pulitzer Prize for *Untitled Subjects* (1969). The entire vol-ume focuses on nineteenth-century figures, with speakers ranging from Ruskin to Richard Strauss to Jane Morris, alongside made-up characters such as an MP's fashionable wife. In Roger McGough's comic 'The Revenge of My Last Duchess' (1999) the envoy to whom the Duke is speaking turns out to be Frà Pandolf's son. Not surpris-ingly, Browning's most significant influence (and Augusta Webster's) lies in the continued vibrancy of the dramatic monologue, which had a notable revival in the 1970s–90s in the work of U. A. Fanthorpe, Jackie Kay and Carol Ann Duffy. Duffy also quotes Browning's 'Home-Thoughts, From Abroad' (1845) as the epigraph to the final poem in her 2005 volume *Rapture*: 'That's the wise thrush; he sings each song twice over, / Lest you should think he never could recap-ture / The first fine careless rapture' (14–16).

The burgeoning discipline of neo-Victorian studies has mostly to date been concerned with the novel rather than poetry. An obvious reason for this is that to pastiche Victorian poetry a contemporary writer must attempt 'neo-Victorian' poetry and few – with the exception of such bravado performances as Howard's – have either the desire or skill to do so. However, one of the now-classic neo-Victorian novels, A. S. Byatt's *Possession* (1990), places Victorian poets at the heart of its plot and features copious amounts of convincing faux-Victorian poetry. A young academic, Roland Michell, alights upon some hitherto undiscovered letters from (invented) Victorian poet Randolph Henry Ash, whose poetry is like Browning's. These letters are addressed to an unknown woman and express the desire to meet her again, evoking the correspondence which started the relationship of Robert Browning and Elizabeth Barrett. The letters turn out to be to a female poet, Christabel LaMotte, who writes poetry that resembles Christina Rossetti crossed with Emily Dickinson. LaMotte is the research interest of another young academic, Maud Bailey, and thus begins a novelistic homage to the excitement of new discovery in literary research. *Possession* is at once detective story, thriller and romance, both in the Victorian past and the novel's present day.

'A Bag of Crisps Beneath the Bough': The best of the rest

It is tempting to imagine Swinburne would be pleased that 'Dolores' (1866) has been co-opted as a character in the role-playing game *Dungeons and Dragons*, and that its refrain – 'Our Lady of Pain' – is the name of an Australian heavy metal band. Hopefully he would be ecstatic that dominatrix Diana Lethaby *mis*-quotes 'A Match' in Sarah Waters' neo-Victorian romp *Tipping the Velvet*. Diana uses *'If you were King of Pleasure . . . and I were Queen of Pain'* (Waters, 1998, p. 239) as part of her seduction routine on the 'handsome' Nan King. Morris, who is often remembered for many other aspects of his life and work as well as being a poet, features in American beat poet and activist Ed Sanders' 'In Praise of William Morris', which opens with the lines 'You have to admit he was groovy, / in the hipster sense (say around 1959) / this William Morris' (Sanders, 2007). Morris is also the subject of Arnold Rattenbury's *Morris Papers* (1996), a poetry collection in which poems are alternatively titled after Morris's wallpapers and writings. Rosie Miles's 'Wallpaper Man (It's Over)' (2012) contains an abundance of Morris references, including many to his poems. Morris also makes a cameo appearance in Alan Moore and Eddie Campbell's cult graphic comic series *From Hell* (1991–6), which explores the Jack the Ripper phenomenon of the late 1880s. Morris reads from his poem *Love is Enough* (1872) to a gathering of socialists as Sir William Gull, Queen Victoria's physician, butchers yet another victim in the street below.

Jewish poet Elaine Feinstein pays tribute to Amy Levy in a poem titled after her (1997), and Wendy Cope has her south-London poet Strugnell attempt his own version of Edward Fitzgerald's translation of the Persian *Rubáiyát of Omar Khayyám* (1859):

Here with a Bag of Crisps beneath the Bough,
A Can of Beer, a Radio – and Thou
Beside me half-asleep in Brockwell Park
And Brockwell Park is Paradise enow.   (9–12; Cope, 1986, p. 63)

Undoubtedly, there is much to parody in Victorian poetry. If twentieth- and twenty-first-century poetry have become much more suspicious of rhyming verse and jaunty rhythms, it is far from the case that rhyme and rhythm have ceased to matter. Victorian poetry and poets remain touchpapers for many contemporary poets, novelists, artists, songwriters and film-makers. In Martin Scorsese's film *Hugo* (2011), the book-loving female lead, Isabelle, claims to have a cat called Christina Rossetti and recites chunks of 'A Birthday'. Perhaps because of the elegiac nature of some of the period's most enduring poems the afterlife of Victorian poetry often registers how we have 'lost' the Victorians – the gap between us and them – and also evokes an imagined lost Englishness. The twentieth-century music of Vaughan Williams, George Butterworth and Gerald Finzi is often regarded as quintessentially English, and all set Victorian poems: Williams mingled Arnold's 'The Scholar Gipsy' and 'Thyrsis' in *An Oxford Elegy* (1952); Butterworth set poems from A. E. Housman's 1896 *A Shropshire Lad* (1911–12); Finzi was repeatedly drawn to Hardy's poems. More recently Elis Pehkonen's *Home from the Sea* (2011) continues this elegiac tradition with a setting of requiem poems by Robert Louis Stevenson. Dennis Potter's play *Blue Remembered Hills* (1984) takes its title from section XL of Housman's *A Shropshire Lad*, and Potter's play is a typically unsettling exploration of lost childhood innocence.

Everywhere in Victorian poetry we see poets wrestling with questions, doubts, uncertainty, change, inner turmoil, death, loss, social unrest, gender inequality and sexual longing. They constantly ask 'who are we?' and 'who am I?' Arnold famously said that 'more and more [hu]mankind will discover that we have to turn to poetry to interpret life for us, to console us, to sustain us' (Arnold, 1987, p. 340) and today bookshops still fill their (usually small) poetry shelves with anthologies to help us through births, deaths, marriages and other memorialized moments of significance. The current British Poet Laureate, Carol Ann Duffy, speaks of sonnets as secular prayers, and many Victorian poets would have understood that sentiment about poetry's heightened focus of attention and absorption. The Victorians' issues may not always be exactly the same as ours, but there is no doubt we still recognize ourselves in their poetry.

Reading and research

- Offer a reading of any Hopkins or Hardy poem that argues for how they bridge Victorian and Modern(ist) poetics.

- Seek out any of the many references here to works which have engaged with Victorian poems and poets. You may also discover new ones!

- What is the work's relationship with the original? Is it interested in the form or metre of the original? Does it make you read the original poem differently?

- Using a Google Image search, or a book on Pre-Raphaelite or Victorian art, or one of the references in this chapter, choose one of the many visual responses to 'The Lady of Shalott'. What moment is being depicted? How does the image 'interpret' the poem? As a representation of a woman what is it saying about gender and sexuality?

- Write your own poetic response to a Victorian poem.

Bibliography

Anthologies of Victorian poetry

Armstrong, Isobel and Joseph Bristow, with Cath Sharrock, eds (1996), *Nineteenth Century Women Poets*. Oxford: Oxford University Press.

Blain, Virginia, ed. (2001), *Victorian Women Poets: An Annotated Anthology*. Harlow: Pearson Longman.

Boos, Florence, ed. (2008), *Working-Class Women Poets in Victorian Britain*. Peterborough, ON: Broadview Press.

Collins, Thomas J. and Vivienne J. Rundle, eds (1999), *The Broadview Anthology of Victorian Poetry and Poetic Theory*. Peterborough, ON: Broadview Press.

Cunningham, Valentine, ed. (2000), *The Victorians: An Anthology of Poetry and Poetics*. Oxford: Blackwell.

Hughes, Linda K., ed. (2001), *New Women Poets: An Anthology*. London: 1890s Society.

Karlin, Daniel, ed. (1997), *The Penguin Book of Victorian Verse*. Harmondsworth: Penguin.

Leighton, Angela and Margaret Reynolds, eds (1995), *Victorian Women Poets: An Anthology*. Oxford: Blackwell.

Maidment, Brian, ed. (1987), *The Poorhouse Fugitives: Self-Taught Poets and Poetry in Victorian Britain*. Manchester: Carcanet.

Negri, Paul, ed. (1999), *English Victorian Poetry: An Anthology*. New York: Dover.

O'Gorman, Francis, ed. (2004), *Victorian Poetry: An Annotated Anthology*. Oxford: Blackwell.

Ricks, Christopher, ed. (1987), *The New Oxford Book of Victorian Verse*. Oxford: Oxford University Press.

Rodensky, Lisa, ed. (2006), *Decadent Poetry from Wilde to Naidu*. London: Penguin.

Thornton, R. K. R. and Marion Thain, eds (1997), *Poetry of the 1890s*, 2nd edn. London: Penguin.

Critical works

Abrams, M. H. (1971 [1953]), *The Mirror and the Lamp: Romantic Theory and the Critical Tradition*. Oxford: Oxford University Press.

Alkalay-Gut, Karen (2000), 'Aesthetic and Decadent Poetry', in *The Cambridge Companion to Victorian Poetry*, ed. Bristow, pp. 228–54. Cambridge: Cambridge University Press.

Anderson, Amanda (1993), *Tainted Souls and Painted Faces: The Rhetoric of Fallenness in Victorian Culture*. Ithaca, NY: Cornell University Press.

Armstrong, Isobel (1972), *Victorian Scrutinies: Reviews of Poetry 1830–1870*. London: Athlone Press.

— (1982), *Language as Living Form in Nineteenth-Century Poetry*. Brighton: Harvester.

— (1987), 'Christina Rossetti: Diary of a Feminist Reading', in *Women Reading Women's Writing*, ed. Sue Roe, pp. 117–37. Brighton: Harvester.

— (1993), *Victorian Poetry: Poetry, Poetics, Politics*. London: Routledge.

— (1995), 'The Gush of the Feminine: How Can We Read Women's Poetry of the Romantic period?', in *Romantic Women Writers: Voices and Countervoices*, ed. Paula R. Feldman and Theresa M. Kelly, pp. 13–32. Hanover, NH: University Press of New England.

— (2004), 'The Victorian Poetry Party', *Victorian Poetry* 42:1, pp. 9–27. Special issue on 'Whither Victorian Poetry?'

Armstrong, Tim, ed. (2009 [1993]), *Thomas Hardy: Selected Poems*. Harlow: Longman.

Arnold, Matthew (1987), *Selected Prose*. London: Penguin Classics.

Arseneau, Mary (1993), 'Incarnation and Interpretation: Christina Rossetti, the Oxford Movement, and "Goblin Market"', *Victorian Poetry* 31:1, pp. 79–93.

Arseneau, Mary, Antony H. Harrison and Lorraine Janzen Kooistra, eds (1999), *The Culture of Christina Rossetti: Female Poetics and Victorian Contexts*. Athens, OH: Ohio University Press.

Attridge, Derek (1995), *Poetic Rhythm: An Introduction*. Cambridge: Cambridge University Press.

Avery, Simon (2011), *Elizabeth Barrett Browning*. Tavistock: Northcote House.

Avery, Simon and Rebecca Stott (2003), *Elizabeth Barrett Browning*. London: Longman.

Bald, M. A. (1923), *Women-Writers of the Nineteenth Century*. Cambridge: Cambridge University Press.

Barrett Browning, Elizabeth (1893), *The Poems of Elizabeth Barrett Browning*. London: Frederick Warne.

Beckman, Linda Hunt (2000), *Amy Levy: Her Life and Letters*. Athens, OH: Ohio University Press.

Beckson, Karl (1987), *Arthur Symons: A Life*. Oxford: Oxford University Press.

Beerbohm, Max (1904), *The Poet's Corner*. London: William Heinemann.

— (1997 [1919]), *Enoch Soames: A Memory of the Eighteen-Nineties*. Privately printed [Lunenburg: Vermont].

Bell, Mackenzie (1898), *Christina Rossetti: A Biographical and Critical Study*. London: Hurst & Blackett.

Benedictus, David (1985), *Floating Down to Camelot*. London: Macdonald.

Benjamin, Walter (2003), 'The Paris of the Second Empire in Baudelaire', in *Walter Benjamin: Selected Writings*, 4, 1938–1940, ed. Howard Eiland and Michael W. Jennings, pp. 3–92. Cambridge, MA: Harvard University Press.

Blain, Virginia (1999), 'Sexual Politics of the (Victorian) Closet; or, No Sex Please – We're Poets', in *Women's Poetry, Late Romantic to Late Victorian: Gender and Genre, 1830–1900*, ed. Isobel Armstrong and Virginia Blain, pp. 135–63. Basingstoke: Macmillan.

— (2001), 'Women poets and the challenge of genre', in *Women and Literature in Britain, 1800–1900*, ed. Joanne Shattock, pp. 162–88. Cambridge: Cambridge University Press.

Bloom, Harold (1973), *The Anxiety of Influence: A Theory of Poetry*. New York: Oxford University Press.

Bloxam, John Francis, ed. (1894), *The Chameleon*. London: Gay & Bird.

Boos, Florence (2000) 'Working-Class Poetry', in *A Companion to Victorian Poetry*, ed. Richard Cronin, Alison Chapman and Antony H. Harrison, pp. 204–28. Oxford: Blackwell.

— ed. (2001), *Victorian Poetry* 39:2. Special issue on 'The Poetics of the Working-Classes'.

— (2002), '"Nurs'd up amongst the scenes I have describ'd": Political Resonances in the Poetry of Working-Class Women', in *The Functions of Victorian Culture at the Present Time*, ed. Christine L. Krueger, pp. 137–56. Athens, OH: Ohio University Press.

Brett-Smith, H. F. B., ed. (1947), *Peacock's 'Four Ages of Poetry'; Shelley's 'Defence of Poetry'; Browning's 'Essay on Shelley'*. Oxford: Basil Blackwell.

Bristow, Joseph ed. (1987), *The Victorian Poet: Poetics and Persona*. London: Croom Helm.

— (1991), *Robert Browning*. New York: St Martin's Press.

— (1993), '"What if to her all this was said?" Dante Gabriel Rossetti and the silencing of "Jenny"', *Essays and Studies* 46, pp. 96–117.

— ed. (1995), *Victorian Women Poets: Emily Brontë, Elizabeth Barrett Browning, Christina Rossetti*. Basingstoke: Macmillan.

— ed. (2000), *The Cambridge Companion to Victorian Poetry*. Cambridge: Cambridge University Press.

— ed. (2005), *The Fin-de-Siècle Poem: English Literary Culture in the 1890s*. Athens, OH: Ohio University Press.

Brown, Susan (1991), 'Economical Representations: Dante Gabriel Rossetti's "Jenny", Augusta Webster's "A Castaway", and the Campaign Against the Contagious Diseases Acts', *Victorian Review* 17:1, pp. 78–95.

— (2000), 'The Victorian Poetess', in *The Cambridge Companion to Victorian Poetry*, ed. Bristow, pp. 180–202. Cambridge: Cambridge University Press.

Burlinson, Kathryn (1998), *Christina Rossetti*. Plymouth: Northcote House.

Byatt, A. S. (1990), *Possession*. London: Chatto & Windus.

Byron, Glennis (2003a), *Dramatic Monologue*. London: Routledge (Critical Idiom).

— (2003b), 'Rethinking the Dramatic Monologue: Victorian Women Poets and Social Critique', in *Victorian Women Poets*, ed. Alison Chapman, pp. 79–98. Cambridge: D.S. Brewer/The English Association.

Carlyle, Thomas (1897), *On Heroes, Hero-Worship and the Heroic in History*, Vol. V of *The Works of Thomas Carlyle*, 30 vols. London: Chapman & Hall.

Carpenter, Mary Wilson (1991), '"Eat me, drink me, love me": The Consumable Female Body in Christina Rossetti's "Goblin Market"', *Victorian Poetry* 29, pp. 415–34.

Chapman, Alison (2000), *The Afterlife of Christina Rossetti*. Basingstoke: Macmillan.

Cheshire, Jim, ed. (2009), *Tennyson Transformed: Alfred Lord Tennyson and Visual Culture*. Farnham: Lund Humphries.

Christ, Carol T. (1975), *The Finer Optic: The Aesthetic of Particularity in Victorian Poetry*. New Haven, CT: Yale University Press.

— (1984), *Victorian and Modern Poetics*. Chicago: University of Chicago Press.

— (2002), 'Introduction: Victorian Poetics', in *A Companion to Victorian Poetry*, ed. Richard Cronin, Alison Chapman and Antony H. Harrison, pp. 1–21. Oxford: Blackwell.

Collins, Deborah L. (1990), *Thomas Hardy and His God: A Liturgy of Unbelief*. Basingstoke: Macmillan.

Connor, Steven (1984), '"Speaking Likenesses": Language and Repetition in Christina Rossetti's "Goblin Market"', *Victorian Poetry* 22:4, pp. 439–48.

Cope, Wendy (1986), *Making Cocoa for Kingsley Amis*. London: Faber & Faber.

Craft, Christopher (1994), *Another Kind of Love: Male Homosexual Desire in English Discourse, 1850–1920*. Berkeley, CA: University of California Press.
Cronin, Richard (2012), *Reading Victorian Poetry*. Chichester: Wiley-Blackwell.
Cronin, Richard, Alison Chapman and Antony H. Harrison, eds (2002), *A Companion to Victorian Poetry*. Oxford: Blackwell.
Cunningham, Valentine (2011), *Victorian Poetry Now: Poets, Poems, Poetics*. Chichester: Wiley-Blackwell.
D'Amico, Diane (1999), *Christina Rossetti: Faith, Gender and Time*. Baton Rouge, LA: Louisiana State University Press.
Disraeli, Benjamin (1981 [1845]), *Sibyl*. Oxford: Oxford University Press.
Dixon Hunt, John, ed. (1970), *'In Memoriam': A Casebook*. London: Macmillan.
Eagleton, Terry (2007), *How to Read a Poem*. Oxford: Blackwell.
Easthope, Antony (1983), *Poetry as Discourse*. London: Methuen.
Eliot, T. S. (1951), 'In Memoriam' (1936), in *Selected Essays*, 3rd edn, pp. 328–38. London: Faber & Faber.
Fanthorpe, U. A. (2010), *New and Collected Poems*. London: Enitharmon Press.
Faulkner, Peter, ed. (1973), *William Morris: The Critical Heritage*. London: Routledge & Kegan Paul.
Feinstein, Elaine (1997), 'Amy Levy', in *Daylight*. Manchester: Carcanet, p. 40.
Felluga, Dino (2002), 'Verse Novel', in *A Companion to Victorian Poetry*, ed. Richard Cronin, Alison Chapman and Antony H. Harrison, pp. 171–86. Oxford: Blackwell.
Forrest-Thomson, Veronica (1978), *Poetic Artifice: A Theory of Twentieth-Century Poetry*. Manchester: Manchester University Press.
Frankel, Nicholas (2000), *Oscar Wilde's Decorated Books*. Ann Arbor, MI: University of Michigan Press.
— (2009), *Masking the Text: Essays on Literature and Mediation in the 1890s*. High Wycombe: The Rivendale Press.
Fredeman, William, ed. (2004), *The Correspondence of Dante Gabriel Rossetti 4. The Chelsea Years, 1863–1872. Part II. 1868–1870*. Cambridge: D.S. Brewer.
Gere, J. A. (1994), *Pre-Raphaelite Drawings in the British Museum*. London: British Museum Press.
Gilbert, Sandra M. and Susan Gubar (1979), *The Madwoman in the Attic: The Woman Writer and the Nineteenth-Century Literary Imagination*. New Haven: Yale University Press.
Gill, Stephen, ed. (1984), *William Wordsworth*. Oxford: Oxford University Press.

Goody, Alex (2006), 'Murder in Mile End: Amy Levy, Jewishness, and the City', *Victorian Literature and Culture* 34, pp. 461–79.

Greenblatt, Stephen, ed. (2006), *The Norton Anthology of English Literature*, 8th edn, Vol. 2. New York: W.W. Norton.

Gregson, Ian (2011), 'Post/Modernist Rhythms and Voices', in *The Cambridge Companion to Twentieth-Century British and Irish Women's Poetry*, ed. Jane Dowson, pp. 9–23. Cambridge: Cambridge University Press.

Hardy, Florence (1994 [1928, 1930]), *The Life of Thomas Hardy*. London: Studio Editions.

Harris, Daniel A. (1984), 'D. G. Rossetti's "Jenny": Sex, Money, and the Interior Monologue', *Victorian Poetry* 22:2, pp. 197–215.

Harvey, Matt (2010), *Where Earwigs Dare*. Totnes: Green Books.

Hawlin, Stefan (2002), *Robert Browning*. London: Routledge.

Heilmann, Ann and Mark Llewellyn (2010), *Neo-Victorianism: The Victorians in the Twenty-First Century, 1999–2009*. Basingstoke: Palgrave Macmillan.

Helsinger, Elizabeth (1991), 'Consumer Power and the Utopia of Desire: Christina Rossetti's "Goblin Market"', *ELH* 58, pp. 903–33.

— (2008), *Poetry and the Pre-Raphaelite Arts: Dante Gabriel Rossetti and William Morris*. London: Yale University Press.

Hetherington, Naomi and Nadia Valman, eds (2010), *Amy Levy: Critical Essays*. Athens, OH: Ohio University Press.

Holdsworth, Roger, ed. (2003 [1974]), 'Introduction' to *Arthur Symons: Selected Writings*. Manchester: Fyfield Books, pp. 9–24.

Holmes, John (2009), *Darwin's Bards: British and American Poetry in the Age of Evolution*. Edinburgh: Edinburgh University Press.

Holt, Terence (1990), '"Men sell not such in any town": Exchange in "Goblin Market"', *Victorian Poetry* 28, pp. 51–67.

Hopkins, Gerard Manley (2002), *The Major Works*, ed. Catherine Phillips. Oxford: Oxford University Press.

Horne, Richard Hengist, ed. (1907 [1844]), *A New Spirit of the Age*. London: Henry Frowde.

Houston, Natalie M. (2002), 'Anthologies and the Making of the Canon', in *A Companion to Victorian Poetry*, ed. Richard Cronin, Alison Chapman and Antony H. Harrison, pp. 361–77. Oxford: Blackwell.

Hughes, Linda K. (2010), *The Cambridge Introduction to Victorian Poetry*. Cambridge: Cambridge University Press.

Johnson, E. D. H. (1952), *The Alien Vision of Victorian Poetry*. Princeton, NJ: Princeton University Press.

Jones, Griff Rhys, ed. (1996), *The Nation's Favourite Poems*. London: BBC Worldwide.

Joyce, James (2000 [1922]), *Ulysses*. London: Penguin.

Jump, John D., ed. (1967), *Tennyson: The Critical Heritage*. London: Routledge & Kegan Paul.

Kaplan, Cora (1978), 'Introduction' to *Aurora Leigh, and Other Poems*, pp. 5–36. London: The Women's Press.

Karlin, Daniel (1985), *The Courtship of Robert Browning and Elizabeth Barrett*. Oxford: Clarendon.

— ed. (1989), *Robert Browning and Elizabeth Barrett: The Courtship Correspondence 1845–1846: A Selection*. Oxford: Clarendon.

Kennedy, David (2007), *Elegy*. London: Routledge.

Kooistra, Lorraine Janzen (1994), 'Modern Markets for "Goblin Market"', *Victorian Poetry* 32:3–4, pp. 249–77.

— (1995), *The Artist as Critic: Bitextuality in Fin-de-Siècle Illustrated Books*. Aldershot: Scolar Press.

— (1999), 'Visualizing the Fantastic Subject: "Goblin Market" and the Gaze', in *The Culture of Christina Rossetti: Female Poetics and Victorian Contexts*, ed. Mary Arseneau, Antony H. Harrison and Lorraine Janzen Kooistra, pp. 137–69. Athens, OH: Ohio University Press.

— (2002a), *Christina Rossetti and Illustration: A Publishing History*. Athens, OH: Ohio University Press.

— (2002b), 'Poetry and Illustration', in *A Companion to Victorian Poetry*, ed. Richard Cronin, Alison Chapman and Antony H. Harrison, pp. 392–418. Oxford: Blackwell.

— (2010), 'From Blake to Beardsley: "On Some of the Characteristics of Modern Poetry"', *Victorian Poetry* 48:1, pp. 1–9.

Krueger, Christine L., ed. (2002), *Functions of Victorian Culture at the Present Time*. Athens, OH: Ohio University Press.

Kunzru, Hari (2011), 'Alan Hollinghurst: *The Stranger's Child*'. Blogpost on: www.harikunzru.com.

Langbaum, Robert (1972 [1957]), *The Poetry of Experience: The Dramatic Monologue in Modern Literary Tradition*. London: Chatto & Windus.

Lasner, Mark Samuels (1999), *A Bibliography of Enoch Soames*. Oxford: The Rivendale Press.

Leighton, Angela (1989), '"Because Men Made the Laws": The Fallen Woman and the Woman Poet', *Victorian Poetry* 27:2, pp. 109–27.

— (1992), *Victorian Women Poets: Writing Against the Heart*. Hemel Hempstead: Harvester Wheatsheaf.

Love, Heather (2007), 'Sister Insider' [review of Sharon Marcus, *Between Women*], *Novel* 41:1, pp. 158–61.

Lysack, Krista (2008), *Come Buy, Come Buy: Shopping and the Culture of Consumption in Victorian Women's Writing*. Athens, OH: Ohio University Press.

Marsh, Jan (1995 [1994]), *Christina Rossetti: A Literary Biography*. London: Pimlico.

— ed. (1994), *Christina Rossetti: Poems and Prose*. London: Everyman.

Matthews, Samantha (2004), *Poetical Remains: Poets' Graves, Bodies, and Books in the Nineteenth Century*. Oxford: Oxford University Press.
Maxwell, Catherine (1997), 'Engendering Vision in the Victorian Male Poet', in *Writing and Victorianism*, ed. J. B. Bullen, pp. 73–103. London: Longman.
McCormack, Jerusha (2005), 'Engendering Tragedy: Toward a Definition of 1890s Poetry', in *The Cambridge Companion to Victorian Poetry*, ed. Bristow, pp. 47–68. Cambridge: Cambridge University Press.
McEwan, Ian (2006 [2005]), *Saturday*. London: Vintage.
McGann, Jerome (1993), *Black Riders: The Visible Language of Modernism*. Princeton, NJ: Princeton University Press.
— (2000), *Dante Gabriel Rossetti and the Game that Must Be Lost*. New Haven: Yale University Press.
— ed. (2003), *Dante Gabriel Rossetti: Collected Poetry and Prose*. New Haven, CT: Yale University Press.
— (2010), 'Literature by Design Since 1790', *Victorian Poetry* 48:1, pp. 11–40.
McSweeney, Kerry (1998), *Supreme Attachments: Studies in Victorian Love Poetry*. Aldershot: Ashgate.
— (2007), *What's the Import? Nineteenth-Century Poems and Contemporary Critical Practice*. Montreal, CA: McGill-Queen's University Press.
Menke, Richard (1999), 'The Political Economy of Fruit', in *The Culture of Christina Rossetti: Female Poetics and Victorian Contexts*, ed. Mary Arseneau, Antony H. Harrison and Lorraine Janzen Kooistra, pp. 105–36. Athens, OH: Ohio University Press.
Mermin, Dorothy (1986), 'The Damsel, the Knight, and the Victorian Woman Poet', *Critical Inquiry* 13, pp. 64–80.
— (1989), *Elizabeth Barrett Browning: The Origins of a New Poetry*. Chicago, IL: University of Chicago Press.
— (1995), '"The fruitful feud of hers and his": Sameness, Difference, and Gender in Victorian Poetry', *Victorian Poetry* 33:1, pp. 149–68.
Michie, Helena (1989), *The Flesh Made Word: Female Figures and Women's Bodies*. New York: Oxford University Press.
Miles, Alfred H., ed. (1891–97), *The Poets and Poetry of the Century*, 10 vols. London: Hutchinson.
Miles, Rosie (1999), 'The Beautiful Book That Was: William Morris and the Gift of *A Book of Verse*', in *William Morris: Centenary Essays*, ed. Peter Faulkner and Peter Preston, pp. 133–43. Exeter: Exeter University Press.
— (2012), 'Wallpaper Man (It's Over)', in *Pre-Raphaelite Poetry*, ed. Serena Trowbridge, pp. 37–9. Birmingham: Pre-Raphaelite Society.

Mill, John Stuart (1986), *Collected Works*, Vol. XXII. Newspaper Writings December 1822–July 1831, eds Ann P. Robson and John M. Robson. Toronto: University of Toronto Press.

— (1989 [1873]), *Autobiography*. London: Penguin.

Morgan, Thaïs E. (2000), 'The Poetry of Victorian Masculinities', in *The Cambridge Companion to Victorian Poetry*, ed. Bristow, pp. 203–27. Cambridge: Cambridge University Press.

Morton, John (2009), *Tennyson among the Novelists*. London: Continuum.

Nagra, Daljit (2007), *Look We Have Coming to Dover!* London: Faber & Faber.

Ormond, Leonée (1993), *Alfred Tennyson: A Literary Life*. Basingstoke: Macmillan.

Page, Norman, ed. (1983), *Tennyson: Interviews and Recollections*. Basingstoke: Macmillan.

Pantechnicon, Rachel (2003), 'Lady of Shalott Day'. Available at: www.rachelpantechnicon.com/poems.html.

Pater, Walter (1986 [1873]), *The Renaissance*, ed. Adam Phillips. Oxford: Oxford University Press.

Pearsall, Cornelia D. J. (2000), 'The Dramatic Monologue', in *The Cambridge Companion to Victorian Poetry*, ed. Bristow, pp. 67–88. Cambridge: Cambridge University Press.

Perry, Seamus (2005), *Alfred Tennyson*. Tavistock: Northcote House.

Pound, Ezra (1954), *Literary Essays of Ezra Pound*, ed. T. S. Eliot. London: Faber & Faber.

Prins, Yopie (1999), *Victorian Sappho*. New Jersey: Princeton University Press.

Ramazani, Jahan (1994), *Poetry of Mourning: The Modern Elegy from Hardy to Heaney*. Chicago, IL: University of Chicago Press.

Rattenbury, Arnold (1996), *Morris Papers*. Nottingham: Shoestring Press.

Rees, Jaspar (2012), 'Opinion: do we really need more classic novels adapted?' 9 January 2012. Available at: www.theartsdesk. com/film/opinion-do-we-really-need-more-classic-novels-adapted.

Reynolds, Margaret, ed. (1996), *Elizabeth Barrett Browning. Aurora Leigh* (Norton Critical Edition). New York: W.W. Norton.

Reynolds, Matthew (2001), *The Realms of Verse: English Poetry in a Time of Nation-Building*. Oxford: Oxford University Press.

Richards, Bernard (2001 [1988]), *English Poetry of the Victorian Period*, 2nd edn. Harlow: Longman.

Ricks, Christopher (1989), *Tennyson*. Basingstoke: Macmillan.

— ed. (2007), *Tennyson: A Selected Edition* (Longman Annotated English Poets). Harlow: Pearson Longman.

Riquelme, John Paul (1999), 'The Modernity of Thomas Hardy's
    Poetry', in *The Cambridge Companion to Thomas Hardy*, ed. Dale
    Kramer, pp. 204–23. Cambridge: Cambridge University Press.
Roberts, Adam (1999), *Romantic and Victorian Long Poems: A Guide*.
    Aldershot: Ashgate.
Sanders, Edward (2007), 'In Praise of William Morris', in *Woodstock
    Journal*. Available at: www.woodstockjournal.com/pdf/morris2.pdf.
Saville, Julia F. (2000), *A Queer Chivalry: The Homoerotic Asceticism
    of Gerard Manley Hopkins*. Charlottesville, VA: University Press of
    Virginia.
Schaffer, Talia and Kathy Alexis Psomiades, eds (1999), *Women and
    British Aestheticism*. Charlottesville, VA: University Press of Virginia.
Scheinberg, Cynthia (2002), *Women's Poetry and Religion in Victorian
    England: Jewish Identity and Christian Culture*. Cambridge:
    Cambridge University Press.
Searching for Alfred: In the Shadow of Tennyson (2009). Introduced by
    Ruth Padel. BBC Radio.
Sedgwick, Eve Kosofsky (1985), *Between Men: English Literature and
    Male Homosocial Desire*. New York: Colombia University Press.
Sharp, Amy (1891), *Victorian Poets*. London: Methuen.
Shelston, Alan, ed. (1971), *Thomas Carlyle: Selected Writings*.
    Harmondsworth: Penguin.
Showalter, Elaine (1992 [1990]), *Sexual Anarchy: Gender and Culture at
    the Fin de Siècle*. London: Virago.
Silver, Anna Krugovoy (2002), *Victorian Literature and the Anorexic
    Body*. Cambridge: Cambridge University Press.
Sinfield, Alan (1977), *Dramatic Monologue*. London: Methuen.
— (1986), *Alfred Tennyson*. Oxford: Basil Blackwell.
Slinn, E. Warwick (2002), 'Dramatic Monologue', in *A Companion to
    Victorian Poetry*, ed. Richard Cronin, Alison Chapman and Antony H.
    Harrison, pp. 80–98. Oxford: Blackwell.
— (2003), *Victorian Poetry as Cultural Critique: The Politics of
    Performative Language*. Charlottesville, VA: University of Virginia
    Press.
Small, Ian, ed. (1979), *The Aesthetes: A Sourcebook*. London:
    Routledge & Kegan Paul.
Snodgrass, Chris (1990), 'Decadent Mythmaking: Arthur Symons on
    Aubrey Beardsley and *Salome*', *Victorian Poetry* 28:3–4,
    pp. 61–109.
Stern, Rebecca F. (2003), '"Adulterations Detected": Food and Fraud in
    Christina Rossetti's "Goblin Market"', *Nineteenth-Century Literature*
    57:4, pp. 477–511.
Stone, Marjorie (1995), *Elizabeth Barrett Browning*. Houndmills:
    Macmillan.

Sussman, Herbert (1995), *Victorian Masculinities: Manhood and Masculine Poetics in Early Victorian Literature and Art*. Cambridge: Cambridge University Press.

Sutphin, Christine, ed. (2000), *Augusta Webster: Portraits and Other Poems*. Ontario, CA: Peterborough.

— (2000), 'Human Tigresses, Fractious Angels, and Nursery Saints: Augusta Webster's "A Castaway" and Victorian Discourses on Prostitution and Women's Sexuality', *Victorian Poetry* 38:4, pp. 511–31.

Symons, Arthur (1924), 'Modernity in Verse', in *The Collected Works of Arthur Symons*, Vol. 8, pp. 44–59. London: Martin Secker.

Taylor, Dennis (1999), 'Hardy as Nineteenth-Century Poet', in *The Cambridge Companion to Thomas Hardy*, ed. Dale Kramer, pp. 183–203. Cambridge: Cambridge University Press.

Tennyson, Hallam (1897), *Alfred Lord Tennyson: A Memoir*, 2 vols. London: Macmillan.

Thain, Marion (2007), 'Poetry', in *The Cambridge Companion to the Fin de Siècle*, ed. Gail Marshall, pp. 223–40. Cambridge: Cambridge University Press.

Thain, Marion and Ana Parejo Vadillo, eds (2006), *Victorian Literature and Culture* 34:2. Special issue on Fin de Siècle Literary Culture and Women Poets.

Thomas, Donald (1990), *The Post-Romantics*. London: Routledge.

Truss, Lynne (2004 [1996]), *Tennyson's Gift*. London: Profile Books.

Tucker, Herbert (2008), *Epic: Britain's Heroic Muse, 1790–1910*. Oxford: Oxford University Press.

Vadillo, Ana Parejo (2005), *Women Poets and Urban Aestheticism: Passengers of Modernity*. Basingstoke: Palgrave Macmillan.

WAG Screen (2009), *The Lady of Shalott*. Dir. Nick Loven. Lincoln. Available at: http://wagscreen.wordpress.com/the-lady-of-shalott-film/.

Waters, Sarah (1998), *Tipping the Velvet*. London: Virago.

Watson, J. R. (1992 [1985]), *English Poetry of the Romantic Period, 1789–1830*, 2nd edn. London: Longman.

Whalen, Terry (1986), *Philip Larkin and English Poetry*. Basingstoke: Macmillan.

Wilde, Oscar (1966), *The Complete Works of Oscar Wilde*, with an Introduction by Vyvyan Holland. London: Collins.

Wildman, Stephen (1995), *Visions of Love and Life: Pre-Raphaelite Art from the Birmingham Collection, England*. Alexandria, VA: Art Services International.

Willson, Judith, ed. (2006), *Out of My Borrowed Books: Poems by Augusta Webster, Mathilde Blind and Amy Levy*. Manchester: Fyfield Books.

Wilson, A. N. (1999), *God's Funeral*. London: John Murray.

Woolf, Virginia (1965a [1932]), 'Aurora Leigh', in *The Common Reader*, 2nd series, pp. 202–13. London: Hogarth Press.

— (1965b [1932]), 'I am Christina Rossetti', in *The Common Reader*, 2nd series, pp. 237–44. London: Hogarth Press.

— (2008), *Selected Essays*, ed. David Bradshaw. Oxford: Oxford University Press.

Yeats, W. B. (1926), *Autobiographies*. London: Macmillan.

Zilboorg, Caroline, ed. (2003), *Richard Aldington & H.D.: Their Lives in Letters, 1918–61*. Manchester: Manchester University Press.

Web resources

The Algernon Charles Swinburne Project: http://webapp1.dlib.indiana.edu/Swinburne/

The Morris Online Edition: http://morrisedition.lib.uiowa.edu/

Poets' Graves: www.poetsgraves.co.uk

The Poetess Archive: http://unixgen.muohio.edu/~poetess/index.html

The Rossetti Archive: www.therossettiarchive.org

Tennyson reading 'The Charge of the Light Brigade' (1890): www.poetryarchive.org/poetryarchive/singlePoet.do?poetId=1569

The Victorian Poetry Network: http://web.uvic.ca/~vicpoet/

The Victorian Web: www.victorianweb.org

The Victorian Women Writers Project: http://webapp1.dlib.indiana.edu/vwwp/welcome.do

The Yellow Nineties Online: www.1890s.ca/

Index